SOUTHERN PACIFIC

Steam Locomotives of the
Southern Pacific Class
Union Pacific Overland Class
Baldwin Experimental 60000

The 4-10-2:

THREE BARRELS OF STEAM

A Complete Collector's File of the Only
Three-Cylinder 4-10-2 Steam
Locomotives Built for Service
in the U.S.A.

Eugene, Oregon May 1949.

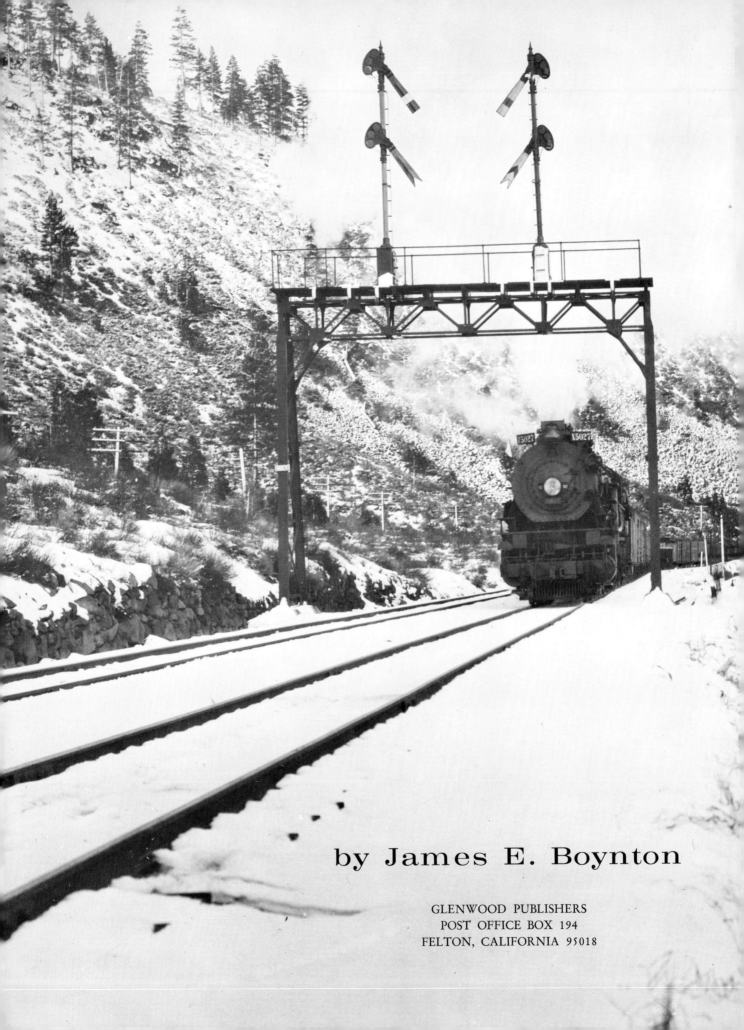

by James E. Boynton

GLENWOOD PUBLISHERS
POST OFFICE BOX 194
FELTON, CALIFORNIA 95018

The 4-10-2:
THREE BARRELS OF STEAM

Printed and bound in the United States of America

FIRST EDITION

ISBN: 911760-13-X

Library of Congress Catalog Card No.: 73-77544

Second Printing

TITLE PAGES

Huge 4-10-2 displays the white flags and indicators of an extra train as she snakes a westbound drag up the canyon of the Truckee River on a cold, bitter winter day in 1930. The three-cylinder locomotives were originally designed and built for both passenger and freight service on the Sacramento Division between Roseville, California and Sparks, Nevada. They were officially designated by the Southern Pacific Railroad as their **Southern Pacific Class,** which encompassed all of that railroad's 4-10-2 wheel arrangement from Class SP-1 through SP-3. Notice that the current of traffic keeps to the left in this photograph.

James E. Boynton Collection.

OPPOSITE — SP 5000 — THE FIRST 4-10-2.

This excellent photograph plainly shows the details of the valve gear arrangement located just ahead of the cylinder saddle. Notice the centrally located cylinder which sloped downward from front to rear at about an 11 degree angle. This was necessary because of its higher placement in the cylinder saddle, while the rear connection of the main rod (center) was about the same level as for the other two cylinders. The throttle rod connection can be seen at the Bradford front-end throttle at the top of the smokebox. Flattened smokebox bottom matches the contour of the cylinder saddle connection. A rounded smokebox bottom on this type of locomotive would have been impossible because of restrictions imposed by the center bore and resultant weakening of the cylinder casting. Photograph taken at Sacramento shops in 1925 by David Joslyn.

Guy L. Dunscomb collection.

Beautifully detailed HO gauge replica of the 5000 series on a section of 90 year old Central Pacific rail. Most of this class were assigned CP initials and the parent railroad existed as a separate entity until June 30, 1959. The watch-like movement of this superb model could quicken the pulse of any boy (mostly big ones) and was built for Westside Model Company of Sunnyvale, California and retailed by Lyman E. Cox Scale Model Trains of Sacramento. The historic length of rail which was rolled only 12 years after the Golden Spike Ceremony at Promontory, Utah, was used on the Boca & Loyalton Railroad and later resold to the Quincy Western Railroad in American Valley of Plumas County.

James E. Boynton photograph.

 This official American Locomotive Company builder's photograph shows details of newly erected **Southern Pacific Class** engine. Number plate between engine truck wheels show that the official order number was S-1495. The original tenders were of the 12-wheel type with a capacity of 12,000 gallons of water and 4,000 gallons of crude oil. Photographed at Schenectady, New York, April 1925.

American Locomotive Company photograph.

Factory fresh 4-10-2 with third cylinder cast in center of cylinder saddle poses outside the Brooks Works of the American Locomotive Company in April 1925. The big experimental was built to burn semi-bituminous coal, but soon had her grates removed. An oil burner was installed in her firebox and 8000 continued to burn ''black gold'' until scrapped as Union Pacific 5090 in 1954.

American Locomotive Company. Gerald M. Best collection.

Contents

Extra 5000 leaving Santa Clara, California in March, 1953 with a string of reefers. The end papers are same date and location as the "off-beat" sounding engine arrived from the San Jose round house.

Charles H. Givens photograph

Foreword

Many of those who follow the beckoning of the iron horse would like to set down in detail, both for their own enjoyment and that of others, the full story of subjects which have captured their interest. Not all are gifted with the ability, the knowledge, the desire and, above all, the dedication to do the job. Because of this, we all often miss the advantage of such a story — our mutual loss.

One more has been preserved, however, with Jim Boynton's treatment of the SP 5000's — in depth with related background and their involvement with history. Whatever needs to be known about them is here, and much may not even have been suspected.

Jim has brought to the subject almost 40 years of intense interest as an admirer and photographer of the steam locomotive, and here is one sharply focused segment of that interest condensed for all to share. Miles of week-end and vacation walking just for the pleasure of seeing this and other subjects have now proved their worth in the latter-day appearance of this record, both for him and for us.

Almost 30 of those years have been spent in engine service; hence a wealth of practical knowledge and experience has been available to create the well-rounded observations of one of his favorite engines.

I very personally share his admiration for the sleek lines of this nearly unique design, still remembering the frustration of not seeing one during the early years of my own interest and the later satisfaction of appreciating and recording them, although never sufficiently. Virtually unchanged in their 25-plus years of existence, the 5000's always commanded a special respect and attention even from those who felt 50-odd look-alikes did not possess the fascination of more individualistic classes— their looks, their voice, their capacity gave them that special niche among the thousands.

And, also very personally, there is the poignant recall of a 7-year-old son who could accept anything I told him about steam engines — except the statement that 5000's had three cylinders. He did want to, but how could that be? So the first sight lives in memory, as he crouched down alongside the 5043 at Bayshore, drank in the details of the center crosshead deep beneath her smokebox, and turned to confirm, "Gee, they *do* have three cylinders!"

Now boy is man and the 5000's nearly all ghosts, only to live in a recollection set to permanent record by one who was marked by their being.

D. S. RICHTER

Preface

It has often been stated with much credance — for every accomplishment there must be a responsible stimuli. It could certainly apply in the case of this photo history of *all* the three-cylinder 4-10-2 type locomotives ever built for service in the United States of America. The image of these curious but beautiful steam locomotives is represented and forever captured between the substantial covers of this 35-year effort. The complete nature of the book proves that continuity does exist for the edification of the serious steam buff.

The original driving force for this documentary was in the form of a steaming, smoking hulk of a 4-10-2 steam breathing *Southern Pacific Class* engine on the head end of a drag freight train in the old Homestead yards of the Southern Pacific Railroad in West Oakland, California. This wonderful event took place in the early 1930's.

Because of its rarity, the three-cylinder 4-10-2 has been fully treated in this publication with all 60 engines included. Long before the advent of the diesel-electrics, my formative years were spent "soaking up" scenes involving these awe-inspiring steam locomotives. It was at this time that I promised myself that I would capture such wonderful memories on film. Vowing eventually to collect photographs of every Southern Pacific 5000 series engine, I found that they roamed a vast geographic range which discouraged such ambitions.

The pleasurable hobby of taking and disseminating steam locomotive photographs was difficult. Most carriers were uncompromising in their attitude toward allowing access to roundhouse facilities; the hobby suffered as a result. After about 25 years of stalking the huge steamers, I found that time was running out as increasing numbers of these "odd balls" were taking up temporary residence at the junk cluttered scrap docks.

The three-cylinder 4-10-2 locomotives were strictly associated with the western United States because only two class A railroads used them and both were part of the original transcontinental link. I soon learned that it would be necessary to enlist the help of several expert collectors to complete this pictorial documentary and it is through their generosity that the book is of such complete nature photowise. Through this cumulative effort and by their mutual cooperation, I was able to complete a pictorial collector's item which includes the silver image of all 4-10-2's built for use in the United States.

The best negatives available of each locomotive were reserved for reproduction in this book. The author has a great debt of gratitude to those who kindly gave of their time and collections so that this record could be entirely complete. Their original desire to preserve the historical images of these immense locomotives is happily shared with the reader.

Guy L. Dunscomb's famous collection was offered unselfishly and includes many famous names devoted to the hobby. *Alan Youell* combed his files and supplied many superb pictures taken by himself and others in the southern California area. Excellent photographs were offered by *Gerald M. Best* from his storehouse of railroadiana. This fine gentleman has no doubt attained the well-earned position as the unofficial Dean of American railroad historians and his numerous publications and papers are with complete authority.

Special thanks to *A. B. Pinnell* and *Andy Wallace* of the Arizona Pioneers' Historical Society who made the fine pictorial coverage of the Bosque explosion available for this book. Much factual data concerning this catastrophe was supplied in Government reports presented by *H. R. Longhurst*, Deputy Director for the Bureau of Railroad Safety. Sincere thanks are extended to *Frank N. Grossman* of the Santa Fe Railroad and *J. G. Shea* of the Southern Pacific Company for their helpful cooperation. *Carl A. Ball*, an old time Southern Pacific locomotive engineer helped develop many of the facts of the Saugus incident through his present assignment at the company's General Offices in San Francisco. It was through *Jimmy* and *Carol Littlefield* that this important data was brought to light after resting in dusty files for over 40 years.

A fine team effort by *Robert* and *Polly Laughlin* assured documentation of the terrible flood of Tehachapi and the wrecking of the West Coast Limited. Without their research and hard digging into old newspaper "morgues," many interesting facets of these stories would be lost forever. It was this helpful allocation of precious time that made the historical facts available. Especial gratitude to *W. Beverly Molony*, a retired "hogger" who lived a life of engine service tooling the three-cylinder giants across the deserts of the great southwest. His true to life excerpts of locomotive operation could only be surpassed by his keen knowledge and ability as one of the old line steam engineers.

To the following I wish to acknowledge and afford recognition for help regardless of how large or small the contribution. The smallest bit of material was large indeed, especially when one missing link spelled the end to a chain of completeness: *Henry Bender, Richard J. Berry, Leon Calloway, Dr. Robert Church, Vince Cipolla, George Corben, Reg and Betty Darby (England), Don Duke, C. E. Felstead, Jack Fesco, Robert Fowler, Robert Hanft, Lewis Harris, Larry Harrison, Paul Herbst, Dave Joslyn, Richard Kindig, Stan Kistler, Elizabeth "Scotty" Lawhern, Thomas Lee, William McKown, Bill Pennington, Otto Perry, Al Phelps, Henry Raub, Doug Richter, Carl Rodolf, Richard Schmeling, Robert Searle, F. C. Smith, Fred Stindt, Walter H. Thrall, Bert Ward, Dudley Westler, Wilbur Whittaker, and Sam Zachery.*

It is at this time that I must register my unremitting gratitude to a patient wife whose kind words instilled and imbued the author with confidence and the will to persist in meeting a great challenge.

Finally, but not in order of importance, a certain group of steam devotees from the Los Angeles confines should be heralded for their optimum efforts to preserve the last of the herd. Through no small desire and effort, they have saved for all time *Southern Pacific 5021*. The results of their timely concern will no doubt thrill some small lad of future generations, a boy who has not been lucky enough to have enjoyed the golden era of steam railroading. I would not hesitate to say that personal involvement in one live excursion behind 5021 would somewhat revive the motivating force that was responsible for the creation of this history in the first place.

Association with the people who helped produce this book soon proved that their responsiveness would make this writing the pleasurable avocation it was intended to be. Without their help this volume would have been impossible to create.

Steam Forever
James E. Boynton

Chapter One

Three Barrels of Steam

At the very inception of the use of steam to power locomotives, railroad men looked forward to larger engines that would haul bigger and heavier trains. Boilers stretched out longer and wider on the drawing boards — this a necessary adjunct to the production of more horsepower. Steam was soon recognized as king of the rails. The evolution of the steam locomotive resulted in many refinements that affected the over-all efficiency of the machine. The most important requirement was power, power, power! Mechanical officers in their preoccupation with designing bigger and better steam engines were prone to accept fads. As they sought out rising tractive effort curves, they knew that the time proven use of expanding steam in two cylinders would have to be revised.

A Swiss locomotive designer, Anatole Mallet, recognized the necessity for more expansion of steam. In 1887 he invented a four-cylinder steam locomotive powering two engines on separate frames. The frames were hinged together so that they could pivot independently, enabling the locomotive to negotiate curves of short radius. Much of the boiler's weight was transmitted to the front engine through a device known as a boiler bearing. This invention, sometimes known as an articulation table, allowed a boiler bearing plate to move laterally on this table mounted on the frame of the front engine. Such an arrangement permitted the forward frame and its engine to move unhindered by the rigidity of the ever-increasing boiler design. No doubt one of the most hair raising experiences witnessed by enginemen new to the Mallet locomotive and mountain railroading was caused by the wide arc the boiler front followed while rounding sharp, tight curves. As viewed from the cab, this frightening scene could very well suggest that the locomotive was about to traverse topography not included in the railroad's original survey.

Mr. Mallet's double engine was of good design and produced the desired increase in power. Restrictive clearances in tunnels, cuts, and on bridges left only one direction open to expanding locomotive sizes and that direction was parallel to the direction of movement. The Mallet met this requirement and latter day designs stretched out into monstrosities which finally evolved into excessive length engines of the Triplex-type. The true Mallet was a double-expansion steam locomotive and in most cases the huge low-pressure cylinders were mounted on the weight-deficient front engine thereby increasing its adhesion to the rail. After the steam was first expanded in the two high-pressure cylinders, it was exhausted into a receiver pipe which conveyed it to the low-pressure cylinders where it was expanded again. This was known as compounding the steam, and engines of this design were known as Mallet Compounds. The double engines came down through the years bearing a perversion of the designer's name and they were almost universally known as Mallies. So impressive was the nickname, nearly every double engine was called a Mallie, and this misnomer was indiscriminately applied to the simple-articulated engines as well.

Most Mallet Compound engines were equipped with an intercepting valve that allowed the engineer to simple or admit steam at boiler pressure to all cylinders by means of a starting valve located in the cab. This was desirable, if not entirely necessary, in starting the heavy over-tonnage trains dreamed up by super enthusiastic railroad operating departments.

During my first experiences running the Mallet Compound locomotives, I was amazed by the tremendous draft that was created at the fire-door when I simpled the big low-pressure cylinders with the starting valve located in the cab. Filled with high-pressure steam, the exhaust really rattled the stack, and the old joke about sucking the fireman or brakeman into the firebox seemed to have substance in fact.

Hundreds of Mallet and articulated-type locomotives were eventually built, some with major differences, but essentially of the four-barrel design.

A few departures boasted six-cylinders, but the four-cylinder design persisted and enjoyed general acceptance on America's railroads.

The simple-articulated locomotives soon became standard equipment on the rail network that spanned the United States and were finally epitomized in the building of Union Pacific's 4-8-8-4 Big Boys. These huge Alco engines were built to tame Sherman Hill near Cheyenne, Wyoming and to boost big tonnage trains over the Wasatch Range in Utah during the golden hour of steam. The Mallies and articulateds were constructed with several wheel arrangements — some with six drivers per engine, but most of the eight-wheel configuration. The blueprints of at least two American class A railroads projected a ten-driver per frame engine.* The three Erie Railroad 2-8-8-8-2 (Baldwin) Triplex Mallets, like the Virginian Railway 2-8-8-8-4, were the only four locomotives equipped with three separate engines — one under the tender frame.

Undoubtedly the strangest Mallet I have ever seen was used on the Great Northern Railway into Bieber, California where that road meets Western Pacific's Northern California Extension. These strange unconventionally arranged locomotives were built with a front engine rolling on six drivers, and a second frame supported by eight. Using Mr. Whyte's formula for official classification of locomotive wheel arrangements, the strange compounds were listed as 2-6-8-0.

Power ratings soar proportionately with an increase in the number of cylinders, a natural result of more voluminous gas expansion. This was an established fact proven long ago by Mallet, and in later years by Rudolf Diesel when he expanded volatile gas in his multi-cylindered "infernal combustion" engines. The standard steam locomotive came down through the years equipped with either two or four-cylinders, and this form persisted with rare exception, until steam power faded into obscurity.

However, American ingenuity was anything but rare, and the dream of a three-cylinder steam locomotive was soon forthcoming. Another fad was unfolding and this new exciting design was graphically shown on the drafting tables of several mainline railroads. The three-bore steam engine was the product of a power-hungry transportation industry. The niche it occupied in railroad history was short at best. Here, definitely, was a hybrid whose number of barrels placed it in a category somewhere between the articulateds and the more numerous two-cylinder engines.

---

* *Santa Fe 3000-3009 (Topeka-Baldwin). Virginian Railway 800-809 (Alco 1918).*

Except for Ephraim Shay's three vertical-bored, power-geared, "slo-go" logging engines, the three-cylinder engine's popularity came and went largely unheralded, and equally unapplauded. Chief mechanical officers had toyed with the three barrel idea for many years, seeking to place their medallions on motive power of extraordinarily high performance. The same general idea persists to this day; motive power officers of modern railroads still seek the ultimate locomotive that can power trains of unlimited tonnage over mountain profiles of terrifying proportions.

A peripheral requirement of this unattainable dream also includes the impossible goal that such power be maintenance free. This seething, moldering problem has plagued railroads since their birth and the closest cooperation with locomotive builders has yet to produce the imaginary perpetual motion machine of infinite horsepower. Progress is often based on such mental wanderings. The search continued and resulted in a natural leaning toward more and bigger cylinders for the exploitation of the increase in steam expansion — simple or compounded.

Historically, the three-cylinder locomotives date back to the early 1840's, but there were no serious attempts to sophisticate the type until 1920. The New York Central Railroad, Lehigh Valley Railroad and the Delaware, Lackawanna & Western Railroad used three-cylinder type 4-6-2 and 4-8-2 engines. The supposed ultimate in steam power was soon projected in the 4-10-2 wheel arrangement, and the American Locomotive Company moved to mass produce the design. Automation of assembly was the keynote of the times, and the locomotive builders were in an advantageous position to meet this challenge.

Only 60 steam locomotives of the 4-10-2 wheel arrangement were ever built for domestic service in the United States, and all of them were equipped with three-cylinders. The largest order ever placed for the three barrel type came in 1925 when the Southern Pacific Company called for the erection of 16. Union Pacific Railroad ordered a pilot model which was assigned road number 8000, and she was completed by Brooks Works of the American Locomotive Company in May 1925 carrying construction number 66169 on her builder's plate. Southern Pacific engine 5000 had been finished in April of the same year, and was assigned shop number 66107. Both locomotives were sent to their respective railroads for testing and then placed in revenue freight service. While engaged in handling fast freight traffic, their performance prompted additional orders which were subject to a very few structural changes over the pilot models.

Sir Nigel Gresley

Sir Nigel (H.N.) Gresley, an extremely dexterous and capable locomotive designer, was Chief Mechanical Engineer for the old Great Northern Railway (England) from 1911 to 1922. The mechanical wizard continued on as the Chief Mechanical Officer for the London & North Eastern Railway which absorbed the Great Northern in 1923 to become one of four great rail giants trussing the British Isles in a web of steam and steel. Gresley's creative imagination took form in the exciting silhouettes of the myriad types of steam locomotives he designed, almost exclusively concentrating on the three-cylinder drive. His drawings called for all classes of engines ranging from shunting (switchers) to banking (helper or pusher engines).

Gresley's great talent culminated in the develpment of his "masterpiece" A-4 class Pacific locomotives. These powerful (T.E. 35,455 pounds) express passenger 4-6-2's were ensconced in a streamlined casing and had 3 (18½" x 26") cylinders supplied with 250 pounds steam pressure. In September 1935, Sir Nigel ordered 35 of these pretty engines and when finally assembled they weighed slightly more than 165 tons, had 80 inch drivers and stretched out over 71 feet of L.N.E. rail.

Two of Gresley's A-4 engines won world wide fame, one disappearing in an explosive flash of unbelievable fury at York, England in June 1942. Caught in the blue-white reflections of the probing and stabbing anti-aircraft searchlights, one of Sir Nigel's favorites found herself the focal point of a tremendous saturation aerial bombardment. By some strange turn of events the passenger engine suffered a direct hit from a screaming bomb loosed by Hermann Goering's Luftwaffe. A "stick" of high capacity explosives bracketed the unlucky 4-6-2 and all hell came loose right in the middle of York. Aided by the internal pressures of her own boiler, the beautiful green passenger engine shuddered and then atomized into a deadly boiling cloud of ugly maroon flame and dust filled steam. The A-4 instantly disintegrated, showering much of York with a rain of shrapnel and other jagged, high velocity missles. The engine's funeral dirge, provided by the wailing air raid sirens, was only a background to the terrific secondary explosions as salvo after salvo whistled into the island fortress.

After what seemed eons, the din subsided and the all clear signal was sounded. The patriotic A-4 was no more, a pitiful pile of junk marking the spot where she stood! Thusly, one of Sir Nigel's "masterpieces" became one of the numerous locomotive casualties of World War II. Train and locomotive "bustin" became a favorite sport for the aerial tactician and many German engine crews were to hear the clatter of 50 cal. armor piercing rounds against their locomotive boilers. Like Gresley's A-4 at York, many of Hitler's steam engines projected their crews toward the "pearly gates" in the same spectacular manner.

More fortunate was Mallard (60022), one of Gresley's record breaking machines that "did it" and happily survived for many years of active service. Singing a song of sweet accomplishment, the A-4 provided a record for a proud nation steeped in the tradition of the rail. On July 3, 1938, with shrill whistle screaming, low hanging exhaust trailing over her seven coaches, Mallard's blurred wheels and valve motion turned up an amazing 126 M.P.H. Mallard proved that this was not a timing accident by maintaining a wonderful speed of 120 M.P.H. for five dazzling miles. Such accomplishments are without parallel and it is difficult to associate a man who built such a speedy locomotive with engines used in American railroad practice.

There was little comparison between Gresley's little English locomotives and the huge three-cylinder 4-10-2's used on the Southern and Union Pacific Railroads in the U.S.A. It was a modification of his valve gear that allowed for the development of the American three-cylinder locomotives, the largest of which were the *Union Pacific Class* 4-12-2's. These ponderous machines (which had the longest rigid driver wheelbase of any steam locomotive ever built) would never approach Mallard's 126 M.P.H. record, nor would the English A-4 grind up a 1% grade with 125 box cars. Gresley's A-4's were lightweights (E&T total 230 tons) compared to the *Union Pacific Class* "Nines" (E&T total 413 tons) but they did share a common third barrel design and the complicated valve gear to go with it. It must be fully recognized that the mechanical ability of the famous English locomotive designer provided much of the technology necessary to develop the three-cylinder locomotive in America.

Big Southern Pacific 4-10-2 proudly posed for Sacramento Shop's official Photographer Dave Joslyn on October 9, 1926. The locomotive is shown equipped with a small, odd-type exhaust deflector, which no doubt evolved into the later universally used "clamshell" exhaust diverter. The engine sports the old, standard Southern Pacific paint job which included a dull gray graphited smokebox, gloss-gray enameled boiler jacket, off-white trimmed wheels with white stars at the driving wheel centers. Shielding over the valve stem extensions kept dirt, sand, water, and other abrasives from cutting the moving parts of the valve gear located just ahead of the piston valve chambers. Staff block-system derrick is fastened to side of cab.

In 1926 the Baldwin Locomotive Works built ten three-cylindered 4-8-2 type engines for the Denver & Rio Grande Western Railroad, and the design came into some favor with the big carriers. The locomotive builders had long used the assembly line technique for producing steam engines, and they all envisaged glowing financial reports due to the acceptance of the revolutionary new type of locomotives.

Although the Union Pacific Railroad waited for results of nearly 13 months of road and dynamometer car testing to prove the 4-10-2's, they felt that 8000's performance justified an order for nine more of the same class. Southern Pacific Company evidently liked the charts turned in by their 5000 and re-ordered seven within a couple of months.

Union Pacific's order for ten of this type locomotive ended their "flyer" involving the experimental-type engine. However, Southern Pacific went on to order a total of 49 which became the largest construction program initiated by an individual railroad.

To honor these never-before locomotives, the American Locomotive Company invited the two carriers to coin a name for them. Southern Pacific Company chose *Southern Pacific Class* and Union Pacific designated their three-cylinder 4-10-2's as the *Overland Class*. The *Southern Pacific Class* engines were used on their Pacific Lines exclusively, and the FTT's of the Union Pacific were eventually assigned to the Los Angeles and Salt Lake portion of their railroad.

Southern Pacific's order, along with the planned appurtenances and allied machinery, was conceived amid the collective mass of convoluting gray matter of the Chief Mechanical Engineer's office and those who staffed the General Superintendent of Motive Power's headquarters on Market Street in downtown San Francisco. As a direct implementation of the brilliant contemplations that transpired at Mr. George McCormick's office, the Sacramento shop drafted plans for the eventual building of 49 of the 220 ton engines. They were to be produced at American's plant at Schenectady, New York.

Steeped in the genius born of years of practical shop experience, the mechanical aggregation had injected the most modern design into their specifications. The resultant three-cylinder miracle was formed in the final assembly of 5000 in April 1925. Ironically, after the delivery of 5048 in 1927, the death knell was forever sounded for one of the strangest "critters" to roam the vast network of Southern Pacific rails. Practical road experience soon pointed up the many bad features incorporated into the design — this becoming very apparent to the men who ran and maintained them. After only

three years of production, changing techniques in carrier management and changes in operating methods dictated a termination to all future construction of these strange experimental engines.

A ponderous non-articulated machine of the single-expansion principle, the *Southern Pacific Class* was a purist's dream from a historical standpoint. The 5000's carried their original road numbers from Alco's erection floor to the very day they reached the big roundhouse in the sky. This was indeed unusual in view of Southern Pacific's constant revamping of locomotive rosters aimed toward accommodating the ever changing motive power scene. By comparison, Union Pacific's 8000 was renumbered two times and the scrappers found it was necessary to burn only two, instead of three, cylinders from her rusting remains.

A near kin to the famous Santa Fe (2-10-2) type, the 4-10-2's had the third cylinder and valve chamber cast into the center of the cylinder saddle. The mechanism that operated the center valve was connected by means of a special Alco patented valve gear which was situated on a perpendicular plane to the regular valve gear. The Alco gear was located between the conventional outer gear frames just ahead of the cylinders and valve chambers. This valve gear was originally designed by H. N. Gresley, an English mechanical engineer. The Alco mechanism derived its motion from the valve stem extensions of the Walschaerts valve gear which was located at its regular placement outside the main frames.

The SP-1, SP-2, and SP-3 class engines of the Southern Pacific Railroad were to become the only three-cylinder locomotives used on the entire system. Needless to say the three barreled 4-10-2's belonged to a closed society; only 60 were ever constructed for use on American railroads. So far, 59 of these huge brutes have been accounted for, and the last one was definitely a one-and-only rarity.

Baldwin Locomotive Works built the experimental 60000 in the early days of 1926. Many serious locomotive historians will question her construction number with good reason. The builder number 60000 belonged in the midst of a group of new locomotives built in May 1927. It is doubtful that the assignment of a jumbled construction number to such an imposing locomotive would add to the glamour of the occasion. The impact of such a well rounded serial number is self-explanatory, and Baldwin officials were prudent, though in error, about the designation of this historic number. The Baldwin 4-10-2 was decidedly different than the other 59 locomotives because it was the only compound 4-10-2 equipped with three-cylinders ever built. Modern competitive techniques made it necessary that Baldwin Locomotive Works enter the market in an effort to capture part of the three-cylinder locomotive sales. Exorbitant driver-axle loadings of the Baldwin model, plus the fact that steam compounding was going out of fashion on American railroads, led to the immediate suspension of construction of any other engines of this type. The Baldwin designed 4-10-2 was outmoded before she left the factory, and though she was never designed with any specific carrier's needs in mind, she later produced outstanding records when tested at Pennsylvania Railroad's Altoona Test Plant, and later as a demonstrator on several railroads.

The 4-10-2's had much appeal to the numerous "engine watchers" of those quondam days of steam. They were a beautiful engine and nothing on rails was prettier than a *Southern Pacific Class* engine resplendent in its glossy black boiler jacket, graphited gray smokebox, and white rimmed wheels with tiny stars embossing their centers. Sight was not the only sense that responded to these beauties. Sound played a great part in their appreciation, and the arrangement of their three-barrels provided a most unusual sound at the smokestack. The three bore engines produced a strange, exotic, off-beat cadence that was never known before, nor was it ever heard again.

The nature of the design placed the locomotives of this class in a spotlight of publicity, especially in the Sacramento, California area where their barking exhausts echoed off the ancient brick walls of the buildings where lurked the ghosts of the Big Four who built the parent road. Many people not associated with the new locomotives became aware of the peculiar stack sounds. The blast of the two outside cylinders, interspersed with the blow from the centrally located barrel, gave the unusual sound, which suggested that perhaps the engines were lame. Some of the old timers described their sound as a hop, skip and jump rhythm, and some "boomer" engineers soon found that the exhausts were of little help in their adjustment of valve cut-off. However, once up to speed, the three-cylinder exhaust became a steady roar much like that of a Mallet or articulated engine and the individual beat at the stack was indistinguishable. This very thing bothered many of the engineers because most of them relied on their ability to audibly monitor the exhausts from the smokestack. Their highly trained ears became very accurate in picking the exhausts apart, thereby determining whether the engine was using the steam expansively and to advantage in respect to overall efficiency. These professional experts were in a majority, but there were some "hog maulers" who operated under the premise that the more noise they made, the better they were doing. It was the latter type engineman who was often found running light engine to the nearest water tank, firebox completely dark and devoid of the sustaining fire — boiler with rapidly drying crown sheet.

The center cylinder, which sloped downward from front to rear at about an 11 degree angle, was crank connected to the second driver wheel axle. The short main rod was afforded the proper clearance on the number one axle which was also cranked to accommodate the center main rod's oscillations. After long years of listening to the normal exhaust of the conventional two-cylinder engines, many engineers operating the 4-10-2's found the exhaust so distorted that it was contingent upon them to consult such refinements as back-pressure gauges, steam pyrometers, etc. which were mounted in the cab. This affront to their natural abilities was often championed in terminal "crying rooms." These scientific encroachments on personal judgment only served to foreshadow the eventual arrival of Diesel's fume spewing "street cars."

The center main rod connection at the number two axle produced endless maintenance problems, and the original strap-type back end with floating bushings was continually being pounded to pieces. The back bushings of the center main rod which fitted over the crank axle of the number two drivers was divided into three parts. Despite the fact that this bushing contained 48 bored holes to provide adequate lubrication, failures were frequent, and the pounding of these engines often aroused the ire of trackside housewives who found mysterious cracks appearing on their most treasured bone china. Repair and breakdown problems were unique because of the between-the-frame location of the third reciprocating engine. Shop forces responsible for valve setting and tramming soon found that most of their working day was to be spent in the dismal pit between the roundhouse rails. This placed the 4-10-2's on limited availability, and the costly upkeep certainly did not paint a rosy picture to the upper echelons. Railroad motive power officers became cognizant of these facts, and were extremely hesitant in adding any appreciable number of three-cylinder locomotives to their equipment rosters.

The *Southern Pacific Class* was first placed in general freight and passenger service on the then maximum 2.6 per cent grade eastward over the snow ridden Donner Summit. The 89 mile ascending grade from Roseville, California to the Summit actually resulted in a vertical elevation of 6,623 feet, and was about as tough a proving ground for locomotives nature could provide. The westbound maximum of 2.3 per cent nearly matched the eastward pull, but it soon became apparent that these engines were much too rigid for the sharp curves over the lofty Sierra Nevada Mountains. Even though an Alco lateral driving box was applied to the first set of drivers, reducing the total rigid driver wheelbase to 16 feet 9 inches, time and experience proved that the mighty SP's were deficient trackwise. The remote and inaccessible lubrication points of the between-the-track machinery produced problems for the engine crews, and the resultant neglect no doubt contributed to many of the innumerable engine failures. While in service on the old Overland Route, they caused much damage to the track by generating extreme values of dynamic augment. The deteriorating center main rod bushings caused terrific pounding which was in turn transmitted to the rail. This tremendous force was also magnified by a change in the delicate balance built into the huge counterweights attached to the number two axle.

Pull? Yes, anything you could tie onto their tails but woe be unto the section foreman who maintained a piece of track over which these beasts roamed.

Although designed principally for dual service on the Sacramento Division, it soon became evident that continued operation of the mountain division would be contingent upon running the big rigid 5000's elsewhere. Later, when taken off the Sacramento Division and assigned to the Western, San Joaquin, Portland and Los Angeles Divisions, they sustained the hopes of their designers by rendering spectacular performances in drag freight service. After years of testing, and some major changes, the center main rod and bearing failures were overcome, to the great relief of all concerned.

I often watched these new giants in the Homestead Yard at West Oakland, California and marvelled at the ease with which they could start 125 loads of sugar beets, weighing nearly 15,000 tons. Immediately after crossing the interlocking at Chestnut Junction, the engineer would "widen" on the big beautiful 4-10-2 and quickly take the heavy train of "gons" up to track speed. The beets were hauled to Alvarado, California where they were processed for conversion to commercial sugar.

The 5000's carried 30 and one half tons on a C-2 type trailer booster. This auxiliary engine added 12,340 pounds tractive effort, which brought the power aggregate to a total of 96,540 pounds. The impressive initial starting power dwarfed the potential of three classes of Southern Pacific Mallet and articulated-type locomotives. More powerful than the 2-8-8-2, 4-6-6-2 and 2-6-6-2 Mallies, the 5000's could gobble the M's like no other single frame engine. At least two articulated consolidation engines had tenders equipped with boosters that added 15,120 pounds tractive effort to their total power production. Southern Pacific engines 4010 and 4028 produced about 10,000 pounds more tractive force than did the 4-10-2's, but Southern Pacific tenders were pooled and the power developed by the locomotive was the prime consideration. In later years many of the locomotive boosters were removed from the *Southern Pacific Class* engines. This is denoted in the roster section of this book by the addition of letter (a) to the official Southern Pacific Locomotive Designations. The booster engines were a constant operating headache, and most engineers preferred not to use them in deference to chancing their very frequent failure and breakdown.

The *Southern Pacific Class* had a total grate area of 89.6 square feet and total evaporative heating surface (steam making) of 5,676 square feet. This liberal application of heat conducting area was sufficient to make steam for the third cylinder, and the locomotives were widely known as free steamers. A 50 unit, type A superheater with a total surface of 1,500 square feet was inserted into the 23 feet 6 inch flues of the boiler and terminated at a header in the smokebox. Most of the auxiliaries were supplied with superheated steam that was piped externally from this header along the upper left side of the boiler to the turret valve just ahead of the cab roof. This valve, also known as the fountain valve, supplied steam to the various globe valves controlling the function of the many devices operated by the enginemen.

The fine steaming qualities of these engines became known to me in later years when I was employed in engine service on the Southern Pacific. I had the opportunity to fire three holers in "chain gang" freight pool service while working on the California Pacific portion of the Western Division. While firing these beautiful engines in the old Cal. P. pool, I found that personal involvement with the 5000's proved they could be "popped" under normal loading conditions without forcing the fire to the point where they would smoke badly. All of the SP's were equipped with the Worthington BL-type feed water heating system, one of several styles that utilized exhaust steam to preheat boiler feed water.

The Bradford front end throttle was employed on this power because of its supposed improved features and the immensity of the 4-10-2's boiler. The throttle valve which was usually installed in the more conventional steam dome was mounted just ahead of the smokestack on these engines. It was in perfect position to receive the superheated steam from the header, and also to provide a smaller pipe volume between the throttle valve and the

Sacramento, California was the original home of this famous-type locomotive, and the huge shops pampered the **Southern Pacific Class.** The 5002 is shown here in mint condition when she was used to handle the huge railway cannon as publicity for a Government bond-selling tour. The engine displays the original factory tender, piston valve extension covers and the typical Sacramento Division exhaust splitter on the stack. The splitter was designed to reduce damaging pressures on tunnel exhaust boards mounted at top inside surfaces of bores and snowsheds. Photograph taken at Sacramento, California, circa 1926.

James E. Boynton collection.

One of the first **Southern Pacific Class** engines as she looked when placed in service on the Sacramento Division. Good planning and design of the locomotive included two cross-compound air compressors which provided engineers with ample supply of air to handle trains of a length that these giants could pull. Roseville, California 1925.

James E. Boynton collection.

A chesty, cigar-smoking Southern Pacific "hogger" looks over running gear as the Fast Mail, train No. 10, pauses at Reno, Nevada late in the year of 1925. Motive power changes were made at Sparks, Nevada, a few miles east of the "biggest little city," where 4-8-2 Class 4300 locomotives were supplied for the fast run across the desert expanse to Ogden, Utah.

James E. Boynton collection.

This extremely rare photograph is perhaps the only service shot of Union Pacific's original venture into the use of three-cylinder steam power. Well known railroad buff and photographer, Otto C. Perry, caught Extra 8000 pulling a 54-car train into Laramie, Wyoming on July 29, 1928. Huge Union Shield — long a Union Pacific trademark — is emblazoned on the side of the 12 wheeled tender.

Richard H Kindig collection.

A low sun illuminates the rarely seen ALCO valve gear which was originally designed in England by Gresley. The valve motion behind the cylinders was of standard Walschaerts design. The round recesses at each end of the pilot beam were known as poling pockets. One end of a stout pole was placed in the pocket, and the other end on a car so it could be shoved in the clear of a fouled switch.

The entire smokebox front was hinged to allow easy access to the exhaust nozzle, flues, superheater elements, steam distribution pipes and the Bradford throttle. Stanchions at end of pilot beam were slotted to accommodate train markers when these engines were making a back-up movement light. Sacramento, California, 1925.

Dave Joslyn photograph. Guy L. Dunscomb collection.

cylinders. This feature reduced the volume of steam supplied to the cylinders after the engineer closed his throttle because the dome-type throttle arrangement necessitated a dry-pipe that extended nearly three quarters the length of the boiler. The additional benefits of such throttle placement was evident to those who had experience using both types. It would only follow that the front end throttle offered a much quicker responding locomotive, which in turn made for better train control.

While running engines equipped with the dome-type throttle valves, I have had the unpleasant experience of having boiler water carry over into the superheater units and immediately flash into many times its volume as steam. Because this water and steam had already passed beyond the main throttle valve, the locomotive became virtually uncontrollable. The runaway could only be regained by "hooking up" the reverse lever to the center position, which blocked off the valves, and then applying the engine brakes to maximum. Lady Luck and running room allowed, I was never involved in more than rough couplings.

The throttle linkage was carried forward along the upper right side of the boiler by means of transfer levers and rods. Compensation for the expansion of the boiler was allowed in the rigging and levers. The boiler, which would lengthen and expand under varying conditions of temperature and pressure, would not cause the throttle to be opened while the engine was standing unattended. The outside throttle arrangement was engineered so that a stretching boiler would close rather than open an unmanned front end throttle equipped locomotive. This good, safe design no doubt forestalled many dangerous runaways in the ensuing years. This positioning of throttle control rods has proven to be unwise in at least one case that is illuminated later in the book involving the wrecking of Southern Pacific locomotive 5042 at Saugus, California. Another very strange feature of this throttle linkage, as designed for Southern Pacific's 4-10-2's, was the fact that one of the transfer rods actually passed through the sand dome. The Lima built Super Power (Class B-1) 2-8-4 type Berkshires, purchased by the Southern Pacific from the Boston and Maine Railroad in August 1945, were the only other series of Southern Pacific steam engines incorporating this unique feature.

In later years a second sand dome was applied to the 4-10-2's allowing the engineer to supply unlimited amounts of grit to the rail, negating the dangerous effects of sliding drivers. A judicious application of sand to the tracks also helped prevent spinning drivers, and the "real estate" piped to the rails also helped eliminate the eventual stalling of heavy trains on slippery mountain grades.

When used as designed for service on the San Francisco Overland Limited, trains Nos. 1 and 2, the 5000's could handle 12 passenger cars and meet schedule commitments easily. The mighty three-cylinder engines could power at least 14 Pullman cars on slower schedules, and, when pressed, could muscle about 950 tons (17 passenger cars) up the eastbound grades of the hill. By comparison, the F Class 2-10-2's of the 3600 and 3700 series could barely handle a dozen cars, and anything in excess of this required a Mikado 2-8-2 helper of the 3200 numberings. If tonnage demands required, two Mikes were used to boost 11 or more "varnish" cars over the nearly 7000-foot high transcontinental line. Fuel requirements were much less for the *Southern Pacific Class* engines, oil burner demands for the three holer engines being logged at nearly 15 per cent less than for other motive power used on the same run.

While the 4-10-2's proved that the mountain grades were no deterrent to their hauling abilities, the aforementioned damage to the track required that they be moved to other divisions with longer sweeps of tangent track. Conversely, the engines were found on every division except the Sacramento — the division for which they were originally designed. The Los Angeles Division welcomed these waifs when they were moved south to a more acceptable environment and they provided exceptional duty in helper and road train service — freight and passenger. Most of them spent their last days plodding the barren desert wastes of the great southwest. When it became obvious that the diesels could eliminate the costly water service departments, these wonderful steam giants took the one way trip to the oxyacetylene torch and ended their days in a spectacular shower of molten metal.

The Union Pacific *Overland Class* led a rather dull existence, wearily hauling trains over the dry, arid regions between Los Angeles and Salt Lake City, Utah. The only relief from these arduous chores was a welcomed water stop under the blazing neon tubes on lower Fremont Street in Las Vegas, Nevada. The Union Pacific 4-10-2's, like their *Southern Pacific Class* cousins, were often seen on the business end of passenger trains, haunting the huge cathedral-like confines of whisper amplifying depots such as served Brigham Young's Mormon migration to the desert heaven in later years. A couple hundred miles south, the reverse was true. The LA and SL initialed giants made their dusty stop at Clark County's seat of Las Vegas where those so inclined could, by virtue of their sinful actions, seek out a much warmer climate than offered by Joseph Smith and his disciples. The FTT's differed much in outward appearance, but were of the same general design. The *Overland Class* employed the dome-type throttle valve, and they used saturated steam in the turret (and also in the manifold on the fireman's side of the boiler head). Perhaps the greatest difference in outward design was the typical extended smokebox which came down through the years as a classic Union Pacific trademark. Although Southern Pacific moved their bells to a location just above the smokebox door, thereby improving their audible range, Union Pacific preferred to have theirs where they were originally installed.

Union Pacific equipped most of their engines with Okadee Company's overhead boiler blowdown system which separated the boiler solids from the steam, dumping the minerals down between the rails. The steam left the centrifugal separator atop the boiler and was blown aloft. Photographic evidence shows alkali staining on the boiler jackets near the firebox and cab on many UP engines. This alone would allow one to conjecture as to the merits of the separating device used with the boiler saving system. The first *Overland* originally burned soft coal of the semi-bituminous variety and none of the FTT's were equipped with a booster engine.

Although the Union Pacific locomotive roster included many three-cylinder 4-12-2's designated as the *Union Pacific Class*, the big transcontinental had a mechanical hierarchy that decided that they had enough of the 4-10-2's and their three oddly placed barrels. In 1942, Union Pacific made plans to rebuild the *Overland Class* and convert them to standard two-cylinder engines. The Los Angeles shops placed huge new two-cylinder castings on the locomotives and then renumbered them to the 5090-5099 series. The metamorphosis which resulted from this major alteration reduced the three-cylinder 4-10-2 inventory on American railroads to 50 locomotives. Despite these dramatic changes in structure, the Union Pacific FTT's assumed their wartime responsibilities with dispatch. If a machine could be regarded as patriotic, these locomotives certainly met the requirements as defined. They spent their last days in helping win World War II, sans their center barrel, boosting the yellow-hued diesels over the tough grade of Cajon Pass in southern California.

Baldwin Locomotive Works was not too happy about the results turned in by actual road testing of their three-cylinder single expansion engines. Their design engineers became inspired to produce the ultimate in steam power and they came up with drawings that resulted in the erection of their 60,000th locomotive in 1926. The 60000 was soon assigned to the Altoona Test Plant of the Pennsylvania Railroad in an attempt to scientifically prove her superiority over single-expansion locomotives.

The radically new type of power was immediately subjected to thousands of miles of static testing. The Altoona Plant, a miracle in itself, was arranged so that the test subject's drivers could turn over on gigantic rollers that absorbed the energy developed by the captive locomotive, thereby simulating actual road conditions. Although steam compounding was exclusive to Baldwin's 4-10-2, the use of a water-tube firebox also set her apart from the other 59 engines of this design. Few roads had used this marine-type firebox, but the higher boiler pressure demanded by the design made it mandatory. Baltimore and Ohio Railroad used this type boiler on many of their locomotives and the Delaware and Hudson Railroad pioneered the water-tube boiler on several of its revolutionary 2-8-0 type "hogs." The elimination of flat firebox surfaces dispensed with the use of the cumbersome staybolts and their attendant maintenance headaches.

Dual valve motions on the right side of the locomotive controlled steam distribution and the valve events for the center (high pressure) cylinder and for the right hand low-pressure barrel. The single valve gear on the left side of the engine actuated the 14 inch piston valve (all around) that admitted steam to and from the other double expansion cylinder. All cylinders were 27 inch diameter and 60000 had a 32 inch stroke all around. The basic theory for building this new type locomotive was to attempt to exploit supposed economies in fuel and steam by the utilization of high boiler pressure and a greater ratio of expansion in the cylinders. The 60000 packed 350 pounds of steam pressure when "skin tight" and her odd shaped firebox contained 100 (four inch) water-tubes. When finally completed, the beautiful new locomotive scaled 457,500 pounds. 338,400 pounds of that total was supported by her 63½ inch drivers.

Tests at Altoona showed that the compound indicated power ratings ranging from 1,500 horsepower to 4,500 which was the maximum capacity of the test plant. It was then assumed that she could have developed horsepower in excess of 4,515 if Pennsylvania Railroad's modern testing facility could have accommodated it. This was very imposing considering that the Southern Pacific 5000's could only produce 3,794 cylinder horsepower by using the Cole formula. But then again, the *Southern Pacific Class* was never scientifically tested on the Altoona test plant, the only fair comparative evaluation of power and efficiency ratings that could have been made.

Baldwin 60000 was used on several railroads as a demonstrator. She was loaned to the following railroads: Atchison, Topeka & Santa Fe — Baltimore & Ohio — Chicago, Burlington & Quincy —

Sacramento was the first home of the 5000 Class locomotives because it was at these famous shops that the 4-10-2's were set up for service. In July, 1925 the Southern Pacific management asked the official photographer at the sprawling shops to furnish good pictures to publicize their new and imposing three-cylinder engines. To record this most auspicious occasion, Photographer Dave Joslyn decided to use a primitive form of "cheese-cake" by posing seven beauties from the popular Fanchon and Marco dancers. Joslyn depicted them as pulling 5004 with filmy ribbons attached to a lovely on the pilot platform. After deep consideration and much debate, Southern Pacific publicity men decided the photographs were much too risque to be used to advertise their new motive power. In view of the changing times and modes, it could be said that for modern purposes the dancers were quite overdressed. Photographs taken at east end of passenger platform of Sacramento passenger depot.

Gerald M. Best collection.

Decorated with the green flags, as First No. 2, the famous Overland Limited, 5004 also affords dancing room for four Fanchon and Marco "hoofers." The engine is equipped with Sacramento Division snowplow which was braced by heavy metal rods bolted to each side of the smokebox.

Gerald M. Best collection.

Union Pacific Railroad 8803 — One of two photographs of this rarely photographed locomotive shows the husky 4-10-2 on the point of a freight train on the approach to Cajon's famous grade. For some unknown reason 8803 evaded the camera of most steam devotees, evidently spending most of her career hauling night trains. The engine is equipped with a headlight dispersion shield which was used in coastal areas during World War II to suppress the beam and hide it from the prying eyes of Japanese submarine commanders. Circa 1942.

Richard L. Schmeling collection.

Great Northern — Southern Pacific. In 1927, Baldwin Locomotive Company dispatched their famous compound to the Southern Pacific shops in Sacramento, California and she was promptly converted to an oil burner. The experimental engine was equipped with their largest tender and was relettered Southern Pacific Lines 60000. The newcomer was then placed in freight and passenger service on the Sacramento Division and was used over the mountain route between Sacramento and Roseville to Sparks, Nevada on the eastern slope of the Sierra Nevada Mountains. She, like the 5000's, quickly demonstrated her proficiency in tearing up the track over Donner Summit, much to the mutual discomfort of Baldwin Locomotive Company and the Southern Pacific Railroad's testing and publicity departments. Southern Pacific, it might be added, was not too enthusiastic about the results produced by Baldwin's super engine power-wise. Tonnage had been regulated so that she never required a helper locomotive, and this falsely led the uninformed to believe that her power was without limit. After many tests on the mountain division, the 60000 was returned to the east, and her last mainline road service was out of Superior, Wisconsin on the Great Northern Railway in January of 1928. She had been converted to burn "black diamonds" again and when the final tally was made, she had only totaled about 100,000 miles in actual revenue road service.

In 1933, Baldwin's 60,000th construction was donated to the Franklin Institute of Philadelphia, Pennsylvania where she resides to this day, no doubt basking in the glory of being the only of her type ever built. This beautiful queen of the rails — and seemingly pampered as such — spent her working days solely as an unwanted demonstrator. Though a room is no place to keep a locomotive, 60000 no doubt still exists by virtue of this very same confinement. Donations of rare steam locomotives have resulted in their prompt conversion to scrap by vandals unless proper protection is afforded by responsible people. The famous Baldwin locomotive was moved into the museum and is supported by special flooring that demonstrates several kinds of bridge construction work. The end wall of the building was sealed and the huge three-cylinder compound began an imprisonment that allowed her only a few feet to move in. Lucky visitors may see this very special "gal" and can take a ride over a short 14 foot transit rigidly imposed by the confines of the end wall of the building. Although lacking the roar of live steam exhaust and the warmth of the throbbing fire, the Franklin Transportation exhibit offers a rare once-in-a-lifetime chance to actually ride a real steam locomotive. The well known museum fastened a huge nut to the frame of 60000 and attached an outsized screw driven by a 15 horsepower electric motor. She only moves about four feet per minute, but this unique exhibit has captured the omnipresent railroad spirit instilled in the more than seven million visitors that have spent a few minutes with her. Contemplate this — 60000 has moved more than 1,000 miles while making her daily run in Franklin's museum!

Of the 60 locomotives in this historic group, only two exist to this day. Southern Pacific 5021 also survives thanks to the generosity of the company's huge railroad and industrial complex and also to the indefatigable efforts of a far sighted group of steam devotees. These fine understanding "iron horse" experts put 5021 out to a rewarding pasture at the Santa Fe roundhouse, San Bernardino, California. Vandals withstanding, she should last for eons with proper care — purely for the edification of those who never heard the methodical beat of "squared valves" and the short cut-off.

This preservation is in itself a fitting memorial to those men who ran and fired the three-cylinder locomotives, and to those who labored so hard in the pit to maintain them for service. Yes, this hulk of an engine, like Franklin's captured Baldwin, is a "rare bird" indeed. Engine 5021 is one of two 4-10-2's left in the world, and is the only three-cylinder single expansion locomotive of the type in existence. Just how exclusive and selective a machine can actually be designed is forever exemplified in this timely preservation of two famous "ole gals."

Chunky convert from Union Pacific three-cylinder design heads an extra freight train at Riverside, California on May 23, 1947. The Worthington feedwater heater has been removed in favor of an exhaust feedwater heater operating on the injector principle and utilizing two sets of nozzles — one for heating feedwater and the other set used for forcing. Trunk of palm tree extends above boiler and appears to project into outer space.

F. C. Smith photograph.

THREE BARRELS OF STEAM

Baldwin Locomotive Works experimental locomotive is shown at Baldwin's factory in Philadelphia, Pennsylvania 1926 — shortly after being built in the City of Brotherly Love. The big 4-10-2 was a compound engine with a high-pressure cylinder powering the between-the-rail gear and two outside cylinders using exhausted low pressure steam from the center barrel. Unlike the American Locomotive Works three-cylinder engines, the valve gear that controlled the center cylinder derived its motion from the right side eccentric link. The water-tube firebox developed a boiler pressure of 350 pounds-per-square inch and the engine produced 82,500 pounds of tractive effort. The 12 wheeled tender held 16 tons of coal and 12,000 gallons of water. The strange appearing dome behind the smoke stack is the front end throttle housing which evidently proved a failure. Later photographs of the locomotive indicate that this throttle was replaced by the American Multiple type.

Herb Broadbelt collection.

Only three-cylinder compound 4-10-2 ever built is shown being moved through the streets of Philadelphia to her final resting place at Franklin Institute Transportation Museum. Notice that the engine has been equipped with another improved throttle valve and still carries the Southern Pacific train indicators.

W. R. Osborne photograph.

Richard H. Kindig collection.

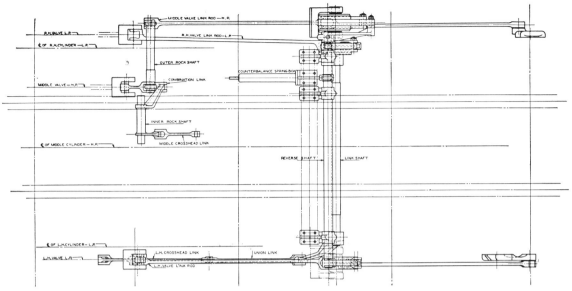

Fig. 13. Plan View of Valve Motion

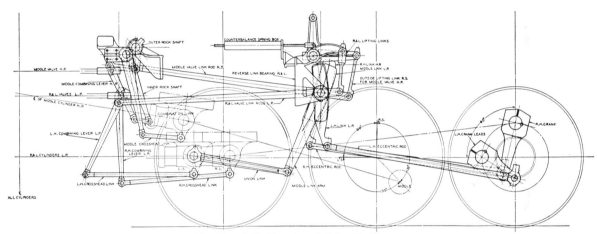

Fig. 13a. Side Elevation of Valve Motion

With silvered smoke box and indicators showing service on Southern Pacific's famous Donner Summit, Baldwin experimental engine has test equipment attached to her pilot platform and also mounted on rear of tender. Dynamo was placed ahead of the stack and pipe along upper right side of boiler indicates use of superheated steam in the turret. The Worthington water pump has been applied close to the source of exhaust steam — reducing loss of heat due to radiation from extended piping. Engine was equipped with a cross-compound air compressor attached to each side of the boiler. Photograph was probably taken at Philadelphia, Pennsylvania after her return to the factory after service as a demonstrator on several railroads.

W. R. Osborne photograph. Richard H. Kindig collection.

Westbound Extra 5046 is shown near San Gabriel, California in May 1933. Stencilled markings on front of the engine indicate last date that the valve settings were made.

Gerald M. Best photograph.

Three-cylinder engine was the subject of much testing to check her steam and draft efficiency. Heavy metal plate mounted on pilot and guard railings protected test personnel who were required to ride the front end of the big 4-10-2 in order to record their findings. Gauges mounted above pilot step near smokebox hinge monitored exhaust nozzle pressure and the steam pressure delivered to the steam chest. Comprehensive analysis of all related data provided guidelines for the proper maintenance and operational techniques for this unique type locomotive. Photograph taken at Los Angeles, California on July 12, 1936.

Allan Youell photograph.

Fast moving SP 4-10-2 is shown roaring through southern California town of Pomona, January 12, 1941 while pulling the second section of train No. 822.

Allan Youell photograph.

Three years after Tom Vernon wrecked her, the 5042 is shown leaving the Taylor yards on train No. 824. The train engine is unidentified, but is also another **Southern Pacific Class** engine. Photographed November 30, 1932.

Gerald M. Best photograph.

Shown on train No. 1, the "Overland Limited," new 4-10-2 is shown looking much as she did when delivered to the Southern Pacific from ALCO. Industrious fireman, armed with long neck oiler, lubricates the bell which was installed to rear of stack. The bells on the first few models were soon moved to a position above the headlight and subsequent orders came from the factory with bells in this more desirable position. Device on side of cab just beneath the arm rest was a crane used to pick up staff hoops. This crane, similar to the device long used to snag mail bags at speed, snared the staff hoop which was used in conjunction with the long outmoded staff block system. Location and date of photograph is unknown although scenery places train somewhere on the Sacramento Division about 1926.

Guy L. Dunscomb collection.

Colton, California was the hideout for many of the three-cylinder locomotives. For many years they were stationed here on the Los Angeles Division and used in train and helper service both ways over Beaumont Summit. The exciting appearance of the 4-10-2's was typical of big Southern Pacific steam power and the class was aptly named to honor the first use of this particular design. Diminutive 2-6-0 (Mogul) class engine 1760 is shown at right side of photograph, probably awaiting assignment to a local freight. Photograph taken about 1936.

Allan Youell photograph.

Southern Pacific Indio helper engine is fastened to front of MT-1 class 4-8-2 passenger engine and helps the west-bound Sunset Limited to top of Beaumont Hill in 1942. Train is pictured at Garnet station where the railroad starts the climb between the San Bernardino and San Jacinto Mountains after crossing the magnificent Coachella Valley. The railroad elevation at Rimlon siding is sea level and 22 feet below this at Indio just west of the Salton Sea. The strange mast fastened to the right side of the regular semaphore signal supports a blue light — an indication that there is another track between signal mast and the track governed by the home and distant block signals. Nearby Palm Springs was soon to blossom into one of the loveliest health and vacation resorts in America but was little more than a remote desert area at this time.

Walter H Thrall photograph. Don Duke collection.

Weary three-cylinder freight engine sits in the siding at Chatsworth, California meeting second section of No. 98, the Daylight Limited on August 18, 1940. Magnificently painted GS-3 engine 4417 holds main track and the beautiful Santa Susana Mountains provide an impressive backdrop to this "never again" scene of steam power in action on Southern Pacific's Santa Barbara Subdivision. It was at Hasson station, a few miles west of this scene that an abortive attempt was made to wreck the Lark passenger train in 1929.

Don Duke photograph.

Bell clanging for a rural road crossing, big muzzled SP-1 engine double-heads train No. 5 at East Pershing Siding, the first siding east of Beaumont Summit. Train engine is a GS Class engine and has been helped by the three-cylinder locomotive over the pass through San Timoteo Canyon of Southern California. Train No. 5 was known as "The Argonaut" and operated between Los Angeles and New Orleans, Louisiana. It was discontinued from Los Angeles to Houston, Texas on June 8, 1958. It was finally discontinued all the way in line with railroad policy to eliminate public passenger service.

W. Beverly Molony photograph.

Big **Southern Pacific Class** engine skims through a field of wild oats as she blasts up Beaumont Hill with a west-bound freight. A laboring helper engine at the rear of the train lifts a column of black smoke as she gives her all in aiding 5027 up the ascending grade of the wide pass through the San Bernardino and San Jacinto Ranges. The mountains rising above the horizon at the left are capped by 11,845 foot Mt. San Gorgonio and the southern margin of the pass is guarded by Mt. San Jacinto which rises 10,805 feet above sea level. Prior to 1948, westbound helpers were stationed at Indio, California but were subsequently moved to Colton, California. Before 1915, all helper trips were made from Beaumont, California and the engine crews worked both sides of the summit which is 2,448 feet above the sea. Photograph taken April 10, 1947.

Frank Peterson photograph. Richard H. Kindig collection.

Speeding freight train is "frozen" by camera as she cuts daisies while pulling second No. 822, a sugar beet drag at Walnut station just west of Pomona, California. The date was July 16, 1947, just about two years after her head-on collision at Redlands, California. Oil dirty face indicates a bell copiously lubricated to overcome its reluctance to ring, a malfunction sure to raise the blood pressure of her crew.

Don Duke photograph.

Two big SP 4-10-2's in pusher service are shown cut into heavy freight train just ahead of a World War II troop car and caboose. The three-cylinder locomotives are helping a westbound drag and are shown at Banning siding which was just east of Beaumont summit on November 24, 1945.

Don Duke photograph.

5016 helps cab forward 4225 on eastbound time freight 992 near El Paso, Texas, circa 1946.

D. S. Richter Collection

A modified three-cylinder 4-10-2 helps train engine 7856, a 4-8-2, up the maximum 3 per cent grades of Cajon Pass with a local passenger train. View was taken near Summit, California and train No. 44 was held down to 15 M.P.H. by a drag freight that was running ahead of the double-header. The nine car train was photographed by veteran rail photographer Richard H. Kindig on June 21, 1946. Notice the west-bound mainline shown at a slightly lower elevation to left of helper engine.

Sailing along at 40 M.P.H., a two-cylinder OVERLAND CLASS engine helps Fairbanks-Morse diesel units 703-702B-707 just north of San Bernardino, California on October 1, 1951. The 14 car passenger train is No. 2, the Los Angeles Limited and the big FTT leads the charge toward the grueling grades of famous Cajon Pass.

Richard H. Kindig photograph.

Last built of the Union Pacific 4-10-2's is shown on a local freight train at Victorville, California about 1946. Train picks up load of rock behind caboose as the fierce afternoon sun blasts this California desert town with furnace like heat. Engine wound up service life at Pocatello, Idaho on November 4, 1949.

Richard L. Schmeling collection.

Road engine 4431, a Lima built 4-8-4, is helped up the grade through San Gorgonio Pass near Ordway station on June 21, 1949. Train No. 2 was the old Sunset Limited which was combined with the Golden State Limited, trains No. 3 and 4 about April 20, 1964. The consolidation was known as the Sunset-Golden State and was renumbered trains 2 and 3. The train was split up at El Paso, Texas — the Golden State moving over the

Chicago, Rock Island and Pacific Railroad to Chicago, Illinois — the Sunset continuing on to New Orleans, Louisiana. In 1969 the I.C.C. gave Southern Pacific and the Rock Island permission to discontinue Golden State portion of run and Southern Pacific immediately renumbered the Sunset Limited Nos. 1 and 2, a three times weekly schedule. Train shown in photograph is adequately powered as evidenced by the clear exhausts of the two big engines.

F. J. Peterson photograph. Don Duke collection.

One of two 4-10-2 locomotives left in the United States, 5021 is shown in her protective coating of gloss enamel at Pomona, California in May 1956. This fine preservation was conducted under the auspices of the Southern California Chapter of the Railway and Locomotive Historical Society. The 5021 is now in storage at San Bernardino, California. Wondrous sound effects of this engine operating under power were recorded in "Whistles West," a phonograph record that was pressed for the Society.

Guy L. Dunscomb collection. Don Duke photograph.

Posed at Los Angeles in November, 1955, during her final days under steam.

W. F. Stewart Photograph
H. Bender Collection

Blasting out of Taylor yard in Los Angeles, 5024 rattles a string of empty refrigerator cars destined to meet the needs of produce shippers in the sunny south. Little was it realized when this picture was taken in January 1933, that this particular engine was to become endowed with the honor of being the last single expansion 4-10-2 type locomotive left in the world.

Gerald M. Best photograph.

5021 in a late appearance on the "hill" at Cape Horn, February, 1950. The 4-10-2 was rebuilt for service on the Modoc Line (Fernley, Nevada to Alturas, California) and was being "run-in" on Donner Summit. A carrier decision moved excess clearance 2-8-8-4 Lima AC-9's from the Rio Grande Division instead.

Al Phelps Photograph

The flat nosed 4-10-2 heading out an extra train slowly enters the yard limits at Colton, California with a train of recently iced refrigerator cars loaded with choice fruit and produce from the sunny west. Low headon exposure to the morning sun vividly accentuates the long transverse lever of the valve gear that controlled the center cylinder. American Locomotive Works built the 10 **Overland Class** locomotive for the Union Pacific Railroad and equipped them with the Worthington feedwater heating system to utilize the waste heat of exhaust steam. Photographs of Union Pacific locomotives bearing their original 8800 numberings are rare indeed and those shown in action in train service situations are far and few between. Picture taken in April of 1939.

Richard L Schmeling collection.

This rare photograph shows 8804 entering the barren desert yard tracks at Yermo, California on March 9, 1940. Engine heads first section of No. 259 and carries green flags indicating a following section of the regular train. Notice baggage car trained just to rear of locomotive.

Don Duke photograph.

The big three-cylinder engines were very rarely found as the focal point of railfan excursions — popular demand usually called for the more glamorous high wheeled passenger locomotives of the 4-8-2 and 4-8-4 design. An exception took place on the Coast Division of the Southern Pacific on March 29, 1953 when freshly painted 5011 powered a fun train during the nostalgic period prior to the end of steam and the use of railroad coaches as the popular mode of travel. The fleet-footed 4-10-2 was caught at Carnadero siding located 83 miles south of San Francisco, California.

Dudley Westler photograph.

Three big **Southern Pacific Class** engines lounge on the garden tracks at the Los Angeles, California roundhouse in May of 1951. All exhibit flared stacks and Pyle-National headlights, but 5020 has bell placed lower than in most applications on this class of engine. Overhead pipes convey steam to garden tracks so that the house-blower connection can be made, allowing fire-lighters to build up steam pressure on dead engines.

Allan Youell photograph.

Gone are the glamour days and the historic designation as one of the famous three-cylinder **Overland** locomotives. This rebuilt FTT carries train No. 154 on her train indicators and has just arrived at Kansas City, Kansas with a "hot shot" time freight. Along with 5093, this two-cylinder conversion was among the last heavy steam road engines used on the Kansas Division prior to complete dieselization. First priority elimination of the expensive water service departments on the L.A. & S.L. caused these engines to be moved to the Nebraska and Kansas Divisions. Last service on the Eastern districts of the Union Pacific was seen between Denver and Cheyenne and Denver and Kansas City, Kansas. Some 4-10-2's were also used between Cheyenne and North Platte, Nebraska and the last used **Overland** saw regular assignment on the Denver to Kansas City turn.

Richard L Schmeling collection.

R. Foster photograph.

Gone are the glory days of leading the brightly enameled diesels through the trials presented by Cajon Pass and its tortuous grades. Here a big FTT spends her last tours of duty prior to re-assignment to the eastern districts, helping passenger trains over the pass. Upper quadrant trainorder signal on mast above cab indicates that no orders are to be delivered to the Los Angeles Limited seen at Summit, California on February 16, 1947.

F. C. Smith photograph.

The heavy gradient of the western mountain ranges required that helper engines be used on most tonnage trains. Here shown are a converted 4-10-2 coupled with a high wheeled 4-8-2 passenger engine cut in ahead of the caboose on a westbound drag out of San Bernardino, California on October 26, 1947. The 4-10-2 is a conversion from three-cylinder design and lasted as such until scrapped at Denver, Colorado in March 1954.

Allan Youell photograph.

After experimenting with the 4-10-2 design, Union Pacific extended the 3-cylinder idea to its largest dimension in the 4-12-2's built in quantity for service on the long but fairly straight Sherman Hill. Council Bluffs, Iowa 1953.

Collection of James E. Boynton

Union Pacific's final answer to Steam to "Flatten" Sherman Hill were the "Big Boys." The 4-8-8-4's were the largest steamers built and moved vast amounts of tonnage. Above, the 4024 and 4005 move 89 cars west at 45 MPH near Lynch, Wyoming, July, 1954. Below, 4007 nearby with 79 cars at 20 MPH in September, 1956.

Tom Lee Photographs

SP's last word in steam was the 4-8-8-2. 4232 is blasting east through Niles Canyon in the Coast Range Mountains East of San Francisco, California, in 1954.

Charles H. Givens Photograph

The 4-10-2 was designed to displace the 2-10-2 on the SP but the 3700's outlasted the 3 holers when diesels came. Los Banos, California 1955.

Charles H. Givens photograph.

Courtesy Sam Zachery.

West Coast Limited's locomotive awaits rescue as relief train with two wreckers stands by on temporary "shoe-fly." Notice displacement of cab in which Engineer Richard Ball was trapped. The wrecking took place between Saugus, California and Honby Station (M.P. 447) on the Mojave Subdivision of the San Joaquin Division. White stains on the boiler and cab indicate areas in contact with escaping high pressure steam. The outside throttle rigging caught onto embankment pulling throttle wide open. The spinning drivers — although terrifying to contemplate — rapidly depleted the boiler pressure — a contributing factor in the engineer's survival.

Chapter Two

Robbery at Saugus

The big three barreled locomotive had just completed the momentary station stop at Saugus, California, and the dull metallic clank of the manhole cover on the big Vanderbilt tender indicated that Fireman Robert C. Fowler had her filled with water. Hands gripping the rear eaves of the cab, Bob dropped down onto the sandbox and then slid across the glossy steel deck to the seatbox on the left side of the big 4-10-2. Engineer Richard C. Ball caught the conductor's tossed lantern signal, released the air brakes, and eased the throttle open, gently taking the slack from the Limited so as not to awaken any of the sleeping passengers. Fowler increased his firing rate to match the blasting exhaust of the accelerating engine, and checked the pulsating needle on his feedwater heater pump gauge, making sure that he was supplying the increasing demand for boiler water. As he overfired, the fire-door rumbled and the damper levers jumped in their retainers but soon settled down as the exhaust smoothed out with increased speed. Ball called across the vibrating cab to Bob, saying to him, "Well Bob, it has been a nice trip so far." Little did the old engineer know that these words were to portend a direct reversal of how things would become.

Although it was one of the many pauses on the scenic run north to Portland, Oregon and Seattle, the importance of this daily occurrence was soon to be eclipsed by an avalanche of sensational newspaper copy. Southern Pacific train No. 59, the West Coast Limited, was soon swallowed by the darkening gloom as she pounded her way toward Mojave, California. The quiet Sunday evening was filled with the strangely haunting off-beat exhaust of the huge dual purpose locomotive. The little knot of humanity leaving the dimly illuminated station platform was suddenly filled with an overwhelming sense of loneliness as the last fading echoes of the beautiful Nathan chime whistle came whispering back from the walls of

Mint Canyon. Engine 5042 had left the Los Angeles, California passenger depot at about 6:30 P.M. with her 12 car train, and the date was November 10, 1929. Bob Fowler had bumped as fireman on the passenger run, and it was his first trip since displacing the regular man. Fowler had failed to show for the run, and Sam Zachery* was called by the crew dispatcher to fire the fast passenger train. Sam Zachery had prepared 5042 for the "varnish" run over the Tehachapi Mountains to Bakersfield, California where the joint Southern Pacific—Atchison, Topeka & Santa Fe Railroad tracks spilled out onto the vast, fertile San Joaquin Valley. Engineer Ball and his emergency fireman were leaving the roundhouse preparatory to moving the big three-cylinder 4-10-2 through the yards to the passenger depot when Bob Fowler showed up for work. In a decision that was later to prove to Zachery's advantage, Sam allowed Fowler to assume his rightful position as fireman on No. 59 that fateful night.

As the train blasted through Saugus yard, the clear green light in the leaving block signal was mirrored on the polished rails as the two enginemen verbally acknowledged the proceed indication. Ball was working 5042 pretty hard now, and was really "knockin' apples" as he tried to get the heavy train back up to track speed and on the "advertised" again. The vivid greenish-yellow beam of the headlight swept the barren hills of the Santa Clara River Canyon, and the last nostalgic sounds of the rumbling train, sounding like distant thunder, rolled back from the mountains giving hint to the uninformed that perhaps a railroad threaded this desolation.

Train No. 59 was now committed to an uneventful journey that crossed the rocky wastes of the ridge and near-desert, and she would soon

Southern Pacific-San Joaquin Division engineer, Seniority No. 1 (1971).

turn north and tackle the heavy grades toward Tehachapi Summit. The activity in the hot spacious cab had settled down to routine chores and the brilliant pulsing glare at the throbbing firedoor reflected from the cluster of brass-bound gauges that covered the sloping back head of the huge boiler. Bob had his fire adjusted at the proper rate to take care of the engine loading now, and both men relaxed in anticipation of the long drag up the heavy grades ahead.

About 7:55 P.M., when they were thundering toward Honby siding, a very strange thing happened. They were running about 25 miles-per-hour because of the tight curves. Engineer Ball had just reached down to make his final adjustment with the reverse lever to regulate his power for speed setting. Fowler made the corresponding change in his fire by means of his oil regulating valve in time to keep the flames from kicking out the fire-door. As the big rigid locomotive eased into a left hand curve, unfamiliar motion gripped the action of the engine. Instantly the engine crew knew something was wrong. As they looked along the length of the huge boiler, the headlight and cylinders danced crazily and a torrential cascade of fire and red hot sparks shot back from under the spinning drivers. As their world fell out from underneath them, 5042 slid onto the ties with an unnerving surge. Instantly the big *Southern Pacific Class* engine proceeded to grind up the track fixtures in an awesome display of fireworks that was more appreciated on the Fourth of July.

In the churning cab the maze of controls was but a blur to the "hogger" who somehow found the H-6 automatic brake valve and quickly placed the handle in emergency position. The response was immediate as the cab filled with the explosive report of the emergency application. Engineer Ball quickly slammed the throttle into the closed position, his gloved hand scribing a vicious arc toward the boiler head. This last violent action was done in the manner well reminiscent of the prize ring tradition. The increasing violence of the three-cylinder locomotive's transit along the ties indicated to the engine crew that she was hellbent to turn herself over. Their suspicions were promptly confirmed as the undulating locomotive gave a sickening roll to the right, throwing Dick Ball into the front corner of his cab. As the right side of the boiler and cab tore into the right-of-way, the impact ripped the cab braces to the boiler loose, and the air was permeated with the acrid odor of hot crude oil and burning steel. Bob Fowler instantly rammed the oil regulating valve, pulling the fire from the boiler, thus eliminating chances of firing the wreckage. In just a matter of seconds, proud, stately train No. 59 was

plunged into serious trouble as the crippled locomotive crunched to rest on her right side in a choking cloud of steam and dust. In an act of self-preservation, the fireman hooked his left leg over his arm rest as the heavy three-cylinder 4-10-2 ploughed into the ballast and his gauntleted hand tightly gripped the grab-iron above the canvas window awning. This calm, cool thinking prevented his falling to the right side of the sliding locomotive, and perhaps from being ground to pulp under the bulk of the 225 ton monster. As the boiler tore into the rising embankment alongside the railroad, the exposed outside front end throttle rigging was caught and pulled rearward causing the huge locomotive's cylinders to again be filled with steam.

The helpless steamer lay with spinning drivers churning away on her right side like a stricken animal in its final death throes. What a fearful sight this must have been . . . a flailing locomotive lying on its boiler, throttle wide open, and with no possible chance for anyone to close it. The whole scene was shrouded in clouds of roaring steam because the boiler blow-off valve had been torn from the right side of the firebox when it ripped into the ground. This powerful jet of high-pressure steam and scalding water was deflected into the cab, seriously burning the trapped engineer. Superheated steam pipes ruptured in the displaced cab, adding their deadly hot vapors of hissing steam to the catastrophe. Dick Ball was in a deadly situation as he found himself trapped between his seatbox and the front of 5042's crushed cab with no route of escape. Fowler clung to the outer surface of the wildly surging cab as the vibrating engine tried to destroy itself in a fit of unregulated frustration. Bob well knew that if he was thrown from his perch into the spinning drivers and lashing valve gear he would be torn into a million pieces.

After what seemed an eternity, the pressures of the boiler fell below the value necessary to power the drivers of the big SP-3 engine, and she finally died, accepting the undignified fate she so little deserved. Bob Fowler then stepped from the sides of the cab across the open gangway and cautiously crawled along the slippery sides of the massive Vanderbuilt tender until he reached the rear end of the huge tank. There on the ground beneath him he recognized Ed Crumply, a deadheading engineer who had come up from the coaches to help the crew of the derailed locomotive. Ed invited the "tallerpot" down to terra again, and in his haste, Bob failed to notice that the canted tender was suspended high above the torn roadbed. As he slid down the rounded sides of the tender at an ever increasing speed, he realized that he was again involved in a desperate situation. Luckily he fell into Crumpley's outstretched arms, and they both staggered to the ties in one of the few amusing incidents associated with this terrible disaster.

Fowler surveyed the accident scene. In the dim glow of the coach lights he could see that the baggage car, smoker and one coach were in the ditch; the first two over on their sides. The rest of the stricken train remained upright by some miraculous stroke of luck, even though the locomotive had destroyed nearly 160 feet of track. The men hurried to the crushed cab with rescue in mind, but the searing clouds of superheated steam made rescue problematical. The piercing screams of the tortured engineer drove them to overcome their discouragment, and after the heat of the roaring steam eased a bit, two waiters from No. 59's dining car used their flashlights to locate Engineer Ball. Fowler and several men who were on the immediate scene then plucked the courageous engineer from the jaws of a horribly painful death. As they emerged from the crumbled vapor-filled cab with the scalded engineer, they were met by Dr. F. H. Campbell of Williams, California who was a passenger on the West Coast Limited.

The doctor helped remove Ball from the wreckage, and then proceeded to administer first aid to his extensive burns. A local Southern Pacific Company surgeon was summoned from Newhall, California and the engine crew was removed to a hospital at Newhall for emergency treatment. Bob was to spend two weeks in the hospital, recuperating at home during the following three weeks. Thorough examination disclosed that Fowler was suffering from a badly burned leg and several dislocated vertebrae. The plucky fireman credited the suction at the fire-door of the wide open throttled 4-10-2 with drawing most of the deadly hot steam from his side of the locomotive. Engineer Ball was not so fortunate. Because the seriousness of his burns required that he again be moved; he was transferred to the White Memorial Hospital in Los Angeles where he was placed under intensive care. Richard Ball started a pain-wracked recovery that cost him ten months of confinement while undergoing treatment for his critically burned body. It is the author's considered opinion that if the throttle rigging on 5042 had not been torn wide open, Ball would have been cooked from his frame before the pressure of the boiler was reduced by the relatively small opening formed by the boiler blow-off valve.

Prior to the arrival of any law enforcement officers, Conductor O. C. French checked his passengers for injuries, and having found none of them hurt, hurried back along the crushed rock ballast to the point of derailment. To his amazement, the dim rays of his lantern outlined a wrench and spike puller where the big SP-3 had first hit the ties. The proof was now positive . . . here lay the tools used to turn the Limited into the embankment at the side of the mainline. The alarm was broadcast, and a rather bizarre case of simple train derailment projected the sleepy little town of Saugus into prominence as the locale of a premeditated train wrecking. Further examination of the track structure indicated to Conductor French that the bolts had been removed from the angle bars that secured the end of the rails together. The bond wires that actuated the block signals had been undisturbed, which proved that the train wrecker knew exactly what he was doing. If he had broken the bond wires, the block signals would have automatically displayed a red aspect, thereby prompting Engineer Ball to stop the Limited before it hit the altered rails.

Subsequent investigation showed that the track had been tampered with prior to the passage of the Owl, a Los Angeles-San Francisco overnight all Pullman train which preceeded the West Coast Limited by about 15 minutes. This fact was borne out by sectionmen who testified that removal of the spikes would take considerably more time than existed between the schedule time of the two passenger trains. It is rather hard to realize, but No. 25 had evidently negotiated the loosened rails with its 15 car train of Pullmans, without anyone knowing how close to disaster they had actually been. The Owl was powered by a 4300 series 4-8-2 Mountain Class locomotive, which was not quite so rigid or heavy as the big 5000 engine. This fact alone saved No. 25 from being wrecked, and from suffering a fate which could quite possibly have been worse than that besetting the West Coast Limited.

Almost before the smoke and dust had cleared, Southern Pacific officials at Los Angeles had word of the wreck. Deputy Sheriff Pember reported that he was an eye-witness to the disastrous accident. The deputy was on a motorcycle on the highway near Saugus, and he was watching the train when it suddenly swerved into the embankment. He obtained aid, and was one of the persons who reached the locomotive in time to assist in the removal of the engineer. Jose Pablo, an employee from a nearby ranch, was asleep in the bunk house at this time, and he was awakened by the rending crash of the derailment. His frantic calls over the telephone brought deputies speeding from the Sheriff's Substation at Newhall.

The frightened passengers spilled from the cars and were shivering in the gloomy darkness alongside the wrecked train. After the initial shock

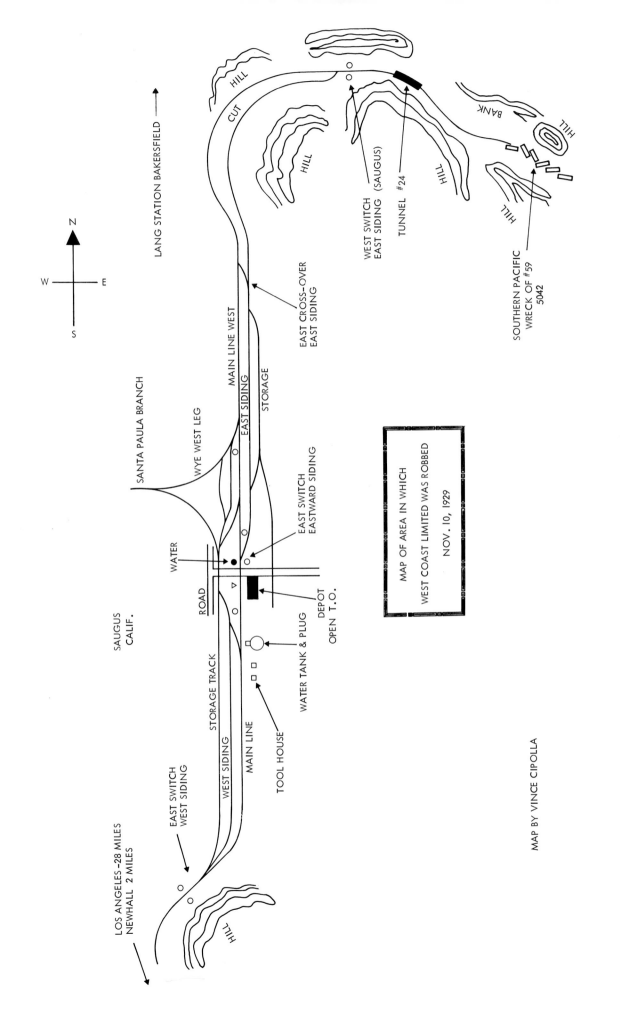

N

W — E

S

LANG STATION BAKERSFIELD →

HILL

CUT

HILL

WEST SWITCH
EAST SIDING (SAUGUS)

TUNNEL #24

HILL

BANK

HILL

HILL

SOUTHERN PACIFIC
WRECK OF #59
5042

MAIN LINE WEST

EAST SIDING

STORAGE

EAST CROSS-OVER
EAST SIDING

SANTA PAULA BRANCH

WYE WEST LEG

EAST SWITCH
EASTWARD SIDING

WATER

ROAD

DEPOT
OPEN T.O.

WATER TANK & PLUG

TOOL HOUSE

MAIN LINE

WEST SIDING

STORAGE TRACK

SAUGUS
CALIF.

EAST SWITCH
WEST SIDING

LOS ANGELES –28 MILES
NEWHALL 2 MILES

HILL

MAP OF AREA IN WHICH
WEST COAST LIMITED WAS ROBBED
NOV. 10, 1929

MAP BY VINCE CIPOLLA

40

of the jolting wreck had somewhat subsided, and the near panic had eased, they were told that the only persons injured were the veteran engineer and fireman. With respect to the primary evidence that this incident was a criminal case of train wrecking, The Southern Pacific Railroad alerted its Chief Special Agent Dan O'Connell in San Francisco and also notified the Police Chief at Burbank, California. About 15 minutes after the train had derailed, the passengers were told to re-train by a nervous little man who seemed to be in authority. He told them that the undamaged portion of the train would soon be pulled back to Saugus by a relief locomotive. Most of the passengers complied in an effort to expedite their return to some semblance of normalcy, and they entered the Pullmans at the rear of the train. Then a most amazing thing happened, much to the chagrin of the excited victims. In a complete reversal from his humanitarian attitude, the man with the professed authority produced an object that left little doubt that he was in complete charge of the situation.

The .38 caliber pistol that he held in his trembling hand added substance to his caustic snarl that this indeed was a robbery. In just a few terror stricken moments it was discovered that a train derailment was to become a criminal act of premeditated wrecking, and now it was being compounded into a dastardly crime of armed robbery. The 15 minute interval between the moment the 5042 rolled over on its side, and the arrival of the hold-up men in the coaches, led to much speculation. The officers were unable to account for this waiting period, except to substantiate that the intent to commit the robbery was a sudden decision made in a deranged mind. The authorities also believed that the train reached the spike-less rails while the wrecker, in a sadistic state of overwhelming joy, stood in the bushes near the track, and happily watched as the engine and cars piled into the ditch. It was only by the grace of God that 5042 negotiated a high fill while bouncing along the ties. If she had plunged off the grade and tumbled down the high embankment, many of the passengers would have probably suffered the same fate as the engine crew, and the casualty list would have been large.

The robber then shoved the short barreled "heater" into the conductor's back, and commanded him to enter the coaches against his will. Being a man with good ability to reason, Conductor French went along with the robber, well realizing that discretionary action negated the possibility of his becoming a prematurely entombed hero. Five persons said they were herded into one coach of the train, and were held quiescent

at pistol point but not robbed. These people were: Mrs. S. E. Brown, Bakersfield; Mrs. Robert Rasmus, Bakersfield; Mrs. H. Schacht, Chicago; Miss Helen Lowe, Chicago; Miss Ann Stowell, Sacramento. The erratic behavior of the bandit proved to benefit Miss Ann Henry, a stenographer from Sacramento who said: "Of course I was terrified, and immediately tore off my rings and handed them to the bandit." He smiled and said: "I don't want 'em lady, keep 'em." Not so fortunate was Mr. Mc Mullen who was standing next to her at this time. Evidently the robber found him much less alluring, but much more interesting than Miss Henry, and this cost Mr. Mc Mullen $30. Dr. Campbell and Dr. W. P. O'Rourke of Seattle, Washington were on errands of mercy which resulted in their being overlooked by the bandit. Both had rushed forward, realizing that crew members and passengers doubtlessly were injured and in need of medical aid. This humanitarian act saved Dr. O'Rouke $100 and the embarrassment of facing the gunman. As the bandit went from victim to victim, an all pervading sense of doom gripped them. The man, wearing a blue bandana handkerchief, waved his gun under their noses with reckless abandon. They had already survived a terrible train wreck, only to find themselves placed in double jeopardy by a five and one-half foot idiot who demanded cash or life.

A lady named Mrs. Hoffman, 74 years of age, was badly frightened by the bandit. "I was sleeping soundly when the wreck awakened me," she declared. "Then all of a sudden the curtains of my berth parted and here was a gun sticking in my face. A gruff voice demanded my money and you can bet I handed him all I could find, which was $25, and as quickly as I could." Pompey J. Anderson, Negro porter, readily admitted that he was "scared." "Ya Sir — Boy ah'm still shaking. Ah never was so glad to see anybody leave in all my life."

This kind of experience was an accepted risk for travelers by railroad in the Jesse James era, but was this not a civilized west now? It was inconceivable that such an amazing event could transpire in this modern world just a few miles removed from the gaudy jungle of lights of one of America's largest cities. Historically, and by custom, these type adventures had been relegated to the dusty files of a conquered wilderness once known as the western plains. It was hard to rationalize that the wild and wooly west had been tamed for many years, especially while being subjected to such indignities as looking down a gun barrel which looked as big as a tunnel bore. So felt Mr. Irwin Bennett, a retired banker from Manchester, England who was enroute to Willows, California to visit his niece. With a reserve tempered by many years of financial decision making, he related in a stentorian voice that: "It was really quite an experience. I had begun to think all these tales of your wild west were fiction, but now I can see they are based on fact. It was my first ride in this part of the country." Mr. Bennett did not so state, but it would involve little speculation to assume that this was his last trip through such uncivilized country.

Incredulous though it was, the robbery progressed and the bandit stated that he was a local rancher and was interested in money only. He kept a running conversation with his victims, and for reasons known only to himself, often removed his cloth mask and exposed his face. The passengers noticed a hole in the pocket of the robber's coat, and through the rent saw another pistol held in reserve. Needless to say, the one held in hand produced the desired result as he moved from person to person extracting their money with much expertness. When the final tally was made, it was disclosed that he had actually robbed 12 persons, and the total loot was between two and three hundred dollars. He had completely ignored jewelry and watches, but did take a woman's purse, which was used to hold his accumulation of illegally procured wealth. Little did he know at this time, but this purse was one of several clues that would eventually ensnare him in a web of evidence that resulted in his prosecution.

Entering one car, the vandal said: "I want currency. Folks, get your money quick. No time! No time! You folks stay where you are, my mate is up at the other end and I left my horse up on the road. I am a rancher here, never mind the jewelry, I want currency."

The reference to the horse injected the Dalton Gang influence into the case and the whole affair assumed the proportions of a Hollywood "flicker." Actually, the passengers described the bandit as possessing a mild, soft voice without a trace of distinguishing accent. They said that he was deeply tanned and was of gaunt, wiry build. He was about 5'6" tall, weighing about 135 pounds, and was thought to be about 40 years of age. He was also described as wearing a two piece suit of brown or grey, the pants being darker than the coat. The passengers said they would be able to identify the man if and when he was captured. There was also a consensus of opinion that the "baddie" had penetrating blue eyes, sunken cheekbones, a sharp thin nose and a smooth face. An opinion was expressed by some in regard to the removal of his mask. Some persons said that he evidently had a subconscious desire to be identified and punished.

Mr. H. E. Pierson, District Passenger Agent for the Southern Pacific, was also one of the robbery victims. Checking the quality of the railroad's passenger service, he soon came to the conclusion that these kind of things were certainly not conducive toward increasing Southern Pacific's passenger traffic. Mr. Pierson placed his business card in his currency hoping that the robber would overlook it, and that it might become a clue as to the identification of the bandit. This quick thinking was to pay dividends when the dragnet was finally formed.

Working his way toward the rear of the train, the nervous gunman came to a locked car door. W. S. Higgins, Southern Pacific employee from Stockton, California was credited by passengers in one car as having saved them from robbery. Higgins was on the train with his wife. Looking outside immediately after the crash, he saw a suspicious looking man running alongside the wrecked Limited, illuminated by the dim reflection of the car lights. Turning away from the window and back to the passengers he cried: "Hide your money and valuables. This is a train robbery." Higgins then had the porter lock the doors at each end of the car and the robber was unable to enter. Among those who profited by Higgins' quick action were Mr. J. W. Maynard, Stockton produce merchant and his wife, and Mrs. J. J. Hooper, wife of a Stockton street car official.

When the bandit found that he could not enter the car, he felt that time ceased to be his ally, and he dropped from the train and melted into the darkness from whence he came. Ironically, the rather small amount of money collected by the bandit was insignificant with respect to the many thousands of dollars that it eventually cost Southern Pacific in damages. His timing was perfect whether intended or not. He was swallowed by the silence of the autumn evening just a few minutes before the deputies raced to the scene. Things were happening fast. On the heels of the deputies came constables from Newhall and police from Central Station, Los Angeles. The alarm for the wrecker was urgently broadcast. After the law enforcement officers arrived on the scene, an intensive search was launched, and all motor roads in the area came under strict surveillance. Due to the fact that the area was so rugged and the night so dark, the search was ineffectual at best, and was called off until the next morning. Southern Pacific officials estimated that the railroad would be opened to traffic in five hours as crews from Los Angeles and Mojave labored to build a temporary "shoe-fly" around the disabled engine and cars. As promised by the bandit, the passengers were taken aboard the last five cars and hauled

Train No. 59's three-cylinder locomotive is shown lying on its right side against embankment after being deliberately wrecked near Saugus, California on the night of November 10, 1929. Fireman Bob Fowler crossed from side of cab to big Vanderbuilt tender and narrowly averted serious injury when he slipped off the rounded sides of the tank to the ground.

Courtesy Robert C. Fowler

View shows front end of **Southern Pacific Class** engine that was pulling train No. 59 near Saugus, California when it was wrecked and robbed by Tom Vernon. Notice mound of earth located just ahead of the 4-10-2's pilot which was ploughed up as the engine slid along on its side. Crude oil seeps into earth underneath locomotive from damaged tender in this photograph taken the day after the reckless crime, November 11, 1929.

Courtesy Robert C. Fowler.

to Burbank where they were dispatched to their destinations by way of the Coast Division. The estimated resumption in rail traffic was accurate, and trains negotiated the new track, by-passing the wreckage. Early Monday morning, November 11, 1929, the trains again ran on the San Joaquin Division. On Tuesday morning the following front page story appeared in the Los Angeles Times:

MIRACULOUS ESCAPE

Railway men marvelled at the miraculous escape of members of the train crew and passengers as the heavy engine swerved from the loosened rails dragging the two cars with it while another left the rails. They state that the slow speed of the Limited approximately 25 miles an hour rounding the curves and pulling the grade in Mint Canyon was the one factor that prevented loss of life and many injuries.

Railway investigators and special men detailed from the sheriff's office after an extensive inquiry gave their combined versions of the wreck and holdup by describing the movements of the train and bandit.

According to the information disclosed, the authorities believe that the affair was carefully planned and carried out by a person familiar with railway construction work.

They believe that the man timed the speed of the Limited for several days prior to the actual wrecking.

This story, written in an obvious attempt to minimize the seriousness of the wreck, gave the engineer and fireman of No. 59 little comfort. Their injuries were all too painful and all too real. Continuing examination of the area disclosed that the tool house near the section shanty had been broken into, and the claw-bar and wrench obtained at about 6:00 P. M. just after darkness mantled the canyons and mountains of the district. The wrecking of the West Coast Limited was almost identical with an effort made the previous Thursday night near Santa Susana on the *Lark*, a San Francisco passenger train that traversed the beautiful California coastline. This attempt was foiled by an alert trackman who discovered the theft of some tools and then traced them to the scene of the wrecking attempt. Mike Smith, trackwalker, found the altered track and tightened the rails before the passage of the Lark. It was believed that another train had negotiated the weakened track prior to the time that Smith had found evidence of the train wrecking attempt. As in the wrecking of the West Coast Limited, a local tool house had been broken into, and the same

type tools were stolen and used in each case. This account of the wrecking attempt was widely circulated by local newspapers and confusion had evidently distorted the actual facts.

As if destined to become a victim of *some* train wrecker, Sam Zachery was nearly put in the ditch near Hasson station a few nights before the West Coast Limited incident. The facts were reported by Zachery who was an eye-witness to the earlier train wrecking attempt. "I don't remember dates too well, but I think it was two nights before this man wrecked the train at Saugus. I had been called with Engineer A. C. Ward up the Coast Division and we had a 2600 or 2700 series 2-8-0 consolidation engine with about 60 freight cars. We were running ahead of a passenger train (I don't remember the number of the train) and were meeting another train at Santa Susana. After passing the train at Santa Susana, it had time to go to Chatsworth against the passenger train. This same man who wrecked No. 59, as he admitted later, broke into the tool house at Hasson and took a spike puller and a wrench. He pulled all the spikes, took the bolts out of the angle bars which left the rail lying loose. The bonding wires remained connected to each end of the loosened rail providing continuity for the signal circuit. As we went over this rail which was loose, it shifted over and our flange hit the next stationary rail. We were told the flange of our locomotive marked the top of this rail for nearly 90 steps, then fell back onto the rail. Our locomotive broke the bond wire when we went over the spikeless rail and actuated a red block signal at both ends of the circuit. After we passed the train at Santa Susana, it had to be preceded by a flagman because of the restrictive signal indication. The alert brakeman found the loose rail and had it repaired so that his train could continue on to Chatsworth to meet the passenger train. Because of the fact that we were running ahead of the passenger train, it was no doubt spared the fate that turned the engine on No. 59 into the ditch." For some strange reason, Sam Zachery seemed to be in the wrong place at the right time, but his formal meeting with destiny was forestalled.

Dan O'Connell, Chief Special Agent for the Southern Pacific Company, arrived at Saugus and marshalled the members of the law agencies and then spread a dragnet over the entire area.*

---

*O'Connell had the reputation of being one of the most able railroad detectives in the country, as it was his untiring efforts that resulted in the capture of the De Autremont brothers. These cold-blooded murderers had stopped train No. 3 in the Siskiyou Mountains of Oregon on October

Derrick lifts smoker which was the second car behind 5042. Derailed locomotive traversed the high fill before turning over — a fortunate aspect of the tragedy. The casualty list would have been very large if the cars and engine had tumbled down the fill. View looks toward Saugus which is about 12 miles from Lang, California where the San Joaquin Valley line was completed from San Francisco to Los Angeles on September 5, 1876. The Baker Ranch and stadium (later the Bonelli Ranch) is in the right background. Photograph taken on November 12, 1929.

Courtesy Robert C. Fowler.

Underside of three-cylinder locomotive is dramatically shown in this "doing it the hard way" scene. The rarely seen counterweights of the center engine are shown at the center of the number 2 driver axle and the wheels and foundation brake rigging show evidence of great abrasion caused when the giant tore up the ballast before turning over. Track in foreground is a temporary "shoe-fly" built in an effort to return traffic to normal and for the eventual rescue of the big passenger engine.

Courtesy Sam Zachery.

After examining the evidence presented to him, Dan came to the conclusion that No. 59 had been wrecked by someone familiar with railroad track work. The most plausible indications were that robbery was intended in both the *Lark* attempt and the actual wrecking of the West Coast Limited. Some people were considering the theory that the crimes were perpetrated by a disgruntled ex-employee of the railroad with intentions of discrediting the railroad as a safe way to travel. It was evident that the wrecker knew exactly what tools to use, and he also knew where to obtain them. As an afterthought, some railroad men said the robber of No. 59 might have been a man who just happened along at the time of the wreck and took advantage of the confusion to carry out his hold-up. Police and sheriff's deputies did not agree with this theory and were certain this was a deliberate wrecking and robbery combined, and the some crime was indicated in the attempt on the *Lark*. The following headline and front page story appeared Monday evening in a Los Angeles newspaper:

POSSES HUNT DESERT FOR
TRAIN WRECKERS
EXPERT TRAILERS TRACE FOOTPRINTS
7 PERSONS NABBED BY POLICE ARE
RELEASED FOLLOWING GRILLINGS

An offer of a reward of $5000.00 for the arrest and conviction of the wreckers and bandits made by

11, 1923. They shot Engineer Sid Bates and Fireman Marion Seng for no other reason than to eliminate the possibility of their identifying them as the robbers. The De Autremonts also killed a brakeman and the baggageman. The baggageman was blown to pieces when he refused to open the sliding door to the mad dog killers. This crime took place at Siskiyou, Oregon on the Old Shasta Route that ran through western Oregon by way of Ashland. After several years of painstaking work, O'Connell wrapped up the case, and the worldwide search was brought to a conclusion which resulted in their incarceration. One of the De Autremont brothers had sought anonymity by joining the United States Army, but this guise was uncovered and his true identity became known. Dan had also captured Roy Gardner, a notorious train robber, arresting him in a Roseville, California saloon. Gardner had robbed train No. 20 near Roseville and O'Connell took him single handed in a cardroom episode in which everyone lost their composure except the robber himself. He remonstrated O'Connell for sticking a "cannon" in his ribs and wisely demanded that the vibrating gun be removed immediately "lest it go off."

the Southern Pacific Company in San Francisco this afternoon was spurring on scores of ranchers, villagers and mountain men in addition to railroad detectives, sheriff's deputies and the like who were already seeking the bandits.

HIRE EXPERT TRAILERS

One posse of expert trailers and trackers led by Pete Le Mere, a veteran Indian hunter, were trying to follow the footprints which led away from the spot where the abandoned coat was picked up. The general belief however was that the bandits fled by motor car soon after getting their insignificant loot.

The all important coat, with the hole in the pocket and a three corner tear on its back, had been found on top of a high hill several hundred yards away from the Baker ranch stadium in which rodeos were often held. The footprints in the dry dust led the posse one-half mile from the train on a path leading directly to the State highway. The jacket had been discarded in hasty flight, and was found crumpled up in a clump of sagebrush. Two hundred yards down the trail the woman's purse was found, along with a business card from the passenger agent who had prudently inserted it in his currency.

The highway soon became the obvious point of escape. Jose Pablo told officers that two automobiles had been parked near the ranch during the day. Clues as to the direction of the bandits' flight came several hours later when a burly truck driver reported that he had seen two men in a Buick roadster hurriedly changing clothes on the Ridge Route. He stated that one of the men matched descriptions of the bandit. A wire was immediately sent to police at Bakersfield and to authorities along the mountain highway. The confusion born from the excitement gave rise to many conflicting stories by the frightened victims of the hold-up. Some of them said that the bandits had gone off together in a single machine. Others felt they had fled in two different automobiles. On Tuesday morning, November 12, 1929 the following headline story was published by the Los Angeles Times.

RAIL BANDIT TRACED
TRAIN WRECKER IN LOS ANGELES
SAUGUS OUTRAGE BELIEVED WORK OF
DEMENTED THRILL HUNTER
POLICE REGARD ROBBERIES AS MERE
AFTERTHOUGHT: ARREST NEAR

Search for a lone bandit who wrecked the Southern Pacific West Coast Limited three miles northeast of Saugus and then robbed a number of passengers of between $200 and $300 was concentrated here last night with an arrest imminent.

Railway detectives, sheriff's officers and police, and ranchers who joined in the intensive quest yesterday to apprehend the vandal responsible for loosening the rails and throwing the engine, baggage-car and smoker into the ditch believed their hunt near an end as the trail narrowed to a single man. Reports from Chief Criminal Deputy Sheriff Frank Dewar, assisted by Captain Brooks who is heading 50 deputies from the sheriff's office and Dan O'Connell, Chief Special Agent for the Railway who arrived on the scene at noon yesterday, indicate that the wreck and hold-up were the diabolical plan of a demented man affected by a mania for vandalism and that the robbery of the passengers was a secondary thought.

REWARD OFFERED

Excellent descriptions of the wanted man and almost certain indications of his escaping from the wreckage scene in an automobile en route to Los Angeles were the basis for the assertion of the officers that daylight will see the end of the chase.

"We have traced the movements of the man from the wreck," Captain Brooks said, "and it will only be a matter of hours before he is in custody. The description of the suspect coincides in almost every detail with the man described by passengers on the train. We are also certain that he is demented," the officer declared. In explaining the belief that the bandit is of unsound mind, Brooks pointed out the conversation and actions of the robber while in the coaches relieving the passengers of only money, and his efforts to engage his victims in a friendly chat. The bandit, according to the officers, wore his mask in one car, removed it in another and then laughingly told the passengers that a relief train would arrive from Saugus in a very short time.

A reward of $10,000 for the arrest and conviction of the man who wrecked the northbound train was posted by the Southern Pacific and United States Post Office Department. Half the amount offered by the railroad and half by the Federal Government.

Engineer Ball who remained at his post as the heavy locomotive ploughed its way over the ties and into the embankment only to be pinned in his cab and suffer from scalding steam was recovering at White Memorial Hospital yesterday. He was the only person injured among the many that were aboard the twelve coach train on its run to Portland and Seattle.

Many clues were being accumulated, and evidence that the modern sleuth was coming into the fore abounded; his equipment encompassing such strange pre-requisites as the microscope, chemical analysis and the all-important College degree. Close examination of the claw-bar turned up fingerprints. The important gray coat was closely examined and a pair of driving gloves was found in one pocket. Inside the gloves, the microscope disclosed metal dust and filings, such as might come from the hand of a workman in iron or steel, or very possibly a railroad section hand. They also found a white handkerchief and a leather key container, clearly indicating to the officers that everything had been discarded in great haste. The hole in the pocket and the three cornered tear on its back, probably caused by contact with barbed wire, was easily identified by the passengers, and gave the investigators positive proof that the coat was worn during the hold-up. Two deputies searching the narrow trail that led from the wreck scene to Saugus found the walk could be made in a mere 15 minutes. They completed the walk without finding any other clues except the purse and Mr. Pierson's business card.

On Wednesday the special agents of the railroad, and the detail from the office of Los Angeles County Sheriff Traeger, under the supervision of Captain Brooks, went into conference on the future course of the chase. It was readily admitted that the robber had cleverly covered his escape, and the search had to split into three directions. The investigators for the Southern Pacific expressed belief that the man sought was a former employee of the railroad at Saugus, who had been discharged several months earlier, and the entire force was proceeding on that premise. Captain Brooks said that his deputies had not only been given a full description of the bandit, but also his name and recent movements, and they would confine their search to the follow-up of clues uncovered late Monday night. As though grasping for straws, a theory was advanced that the man sought was an escaped inmate of the California State Narcotic Hospital at Spadra, California.

"We are sure that the man who wrecked the train was a former ranch employee," Captain Brooks said. "We have determined that the coat found near the wreck on Monday morning belonged to this man and that he was known to be slightly demented and that he suddenly disappeared. Just before the wreck the coat was missing from the bunk house at the ranch where it had been hanging and had been thrown away by the bandit." Conductor French had positively identified the coat as being worn by the desperado, and his close proximity to him during the commission of the crime made this clue extremely important.

Leads were coming in from every quarter. A clue to the identity of the robber was given by W. E. Bradford from Long Beach, California. Bradford told investigators that he overheard a conversation in the washroom at the Saugus railway station between two men who were discussing the best means of derailing a train. This occurred nine days prior to the derailment of train No. 59. "There were two men," Bradford was quoted as saying; "One of them weighed about 170 pounds, was about 34 years of age and was dressed in a worn blue suit. The other character was about five feet six inches tall, slender build, sandy hair and wore a gray sweater and gray coat. They were talking together about how they would pull out spikes, derail the train and then rob the passengers. I had nearly $200 in gold in my pocket and I was going to give it to my wife for a birthday present, but I left as soon as I could, fearing they might hold me up."

The sheriff's deputies said the description of the second man tallied closely with the person picked up on the highway near the scene of the wreck. Captain Brooks said his men had investigated dozens of reports of mysterious cars parked near the Baker ranch, where the train was wrecked, and had combed the haunts of the moving picture cowboys in Hollywood. This "angle" was followed without producing any concrete results.

The ever present sensationalism of the case took on the proportions of Hollywood's favorite theme, the "horse opera," and this was proven by the following story published in the Los Angeles Evening Express dated Tuesday, November 12, 1929.

S. P. WRECKERS HUNTED IN AIR DESPERADOES WHO RIFLED TRAIN ARE BELIEVED IN VASQUEZ ROCKS

An airplane search of the region in which are located the historic Vasquez Rocks — once the stronghold of the notorious train robber and stage coach bandit of that name, was to be made by sheriff's deputies in locating the man or men who Sunday night held up the West Coast Limited.

From a ranch near the fastness of great tumbled stones came word this morning that during two or three recent days two men had been observed transporting provisions over the most impassable mountain trail leading to Vasquez's stronghold.

IS NEAR SAUGUS

The famous rocks are eight or ten miles from Saugus where the train was derailed. One or two armed men could almost defy an army if given the protection of the great stones. Deputy sheriff Frank Dewar who was in charge at Saugus this morning decided to have his men fly over the region both for reasons of safety and because it would take days to search the area afoot. Mr. and Mrs. W. L. McCullum who live on a ranch near Lang, California midway between the scene of the train robbery and the Vasquez Rocks reported that for three days recent, two men, one of them answering the general description, had been engaged in packing something into the district. Each day the pair drove a loaded auto to a spot on a little used road in Soledad Canyon leaving it parked there for almost a day at a time indicating a long trek into the back country. They appeared to carry in provisions and came back empty handed.

A former Southern Pacific Co. employee believed to be mentally unbalanced was being sought in the vicinity of the line's Los Angeles yards and shop as the wrecker and robber of the West Coast Limited.

Imaginations were running rampant, and reports flooded the officers, only adding distraction to an already complicated case. The gray coat remained the most important clue, and was soon subjected to minute scrutiny. Laboratory examination turned up a blurred cleaner's mark in the lining of the coat that appeared partially legible. This sent the deputies combing the dry cleaning establishments of the county, but they came up with no information about the ownership of the coat. Another label was found on the coat which proved to be the No. 1 red-hot clue, because it advertised the fact that the jacket had been made by a Cincinnati, Ohio tailoring firm. With this information in hand, officers soon launched an intensive effort to learn the identity of the coat's owner. The legal snare was slowly being formed, and officers soon uncovered an amazing story of lies and intrigue.

Thomas Frith of Burbank was driving past the wreck scene with his wife and two daughters. They had been out for a drive on the desert east of Saugus and had stopped at the little mountain town for gasoline. As they waited for the attendant to hand pump the fluid up into the heavy glass bowl atop the metal pump stand, a rather anxious individual approached and tapped on the window of their car. The stranger said his little girl had been injured in the train wreck and had been taken to the hospital in Hollywood. He asked them to drive him there. Touched with compassion, Frith picked up the stranger and without going to visit the scene of the wreck, proceeded to Hollywood on his intended errand of mercy. Speeding southward, the Friths were soon confused by a barrage of untruths and fabrications that made their heads swim. The stranger, evidently in a state of great confusion, changed his story several times in an apparent effort to appeal to the emotional nature of his considerate hosts.

The newly acquired passenger told Frith his name was Hall, and that he was a forest ranger on patrol when he came upon the wreck quite innocently. He first said that he had gone to Los Angeles to put his daughter on the West Coast Limited in care of the conductor. He then said that his little 11-year old girl got on the train by herself, and that the serious injuries she suffered in the derailment necessitated his immediate return to Hollywood. The lies were coming fast and furiously, and Hall told how he was riding his horse on the hill behind the scene of the wreck, and when he saw the wrecked train, he tried to ride his horse down to the railroad. He said that he was unable to make it down to the wreck and he lost his gun, badge, and finally had to take his coat off. He told of how the train was wrecked by a person who took the spikes from the rails and unbolted the angle bars that held them together. He also described the vivid scenes around the wrecked cars when the passengers were robbed. It seemed to the Friths that this character knew too much of the intimate details associated with the crime, and took note of the man's appearance. They later found that his description corresponded in many ways with that broadcast by the officers investigating the wreck and robbery. Frith said his mysterious guest wore a blue shirt and dark gray hat, had light blue eyes and was about five feet six inches tall.

Hall again laced his story with distortion, changing it by telling the Friths that his horse first sensed the wreck. According to Hall, the horse had "spooked," causing him to seek out the reason, which resulted in his locating the wrecked train. Overcome by the ghastly scene, and by the fact that his daughter was on the train, he left his coat and horse on the hillside, and hurried to the wreck in an effort to locate his daughter. Mr. Frith, who was employed in the motion picture industry, felt somewhat akin to the stranger because of his talented imagination. There seemed no doubt that this man possessed a talent that was complimentary to the "flickers." After a short period of interrogation, the stranger again gave the details of the robbery. He then reversed the trend and asked Frith if he knew any cowboys who were appearing in the movies. He informed Frith that he had worked with many of them in rodeos and stock shows, and that they were good friends of his. Hall inferred that he was a native of Wyoming and had worked his way west via shows at Yellowstone,

Pendleton, Oregon and several other cow-towns. He also mentioned that he had an operation for appendicitis and was sent to Santa Barbara and thence to Saugus. He never did divulge why he was sent to this part of the state or by whom.

Upon arrival at Hollywood Children's Hospital, Hall tendered the Frith family a $5 bill as payment for the ride from Saugus. The Friths said they would remain outside the hospital until they learned of the little girl's condition. Hall then walked down the driveway, into the hospital, returning in about five minutes with his report about the girl. Hall stated that his daughter suffered fractures of both arms, but that her head was not crushed as he was led to believe. When asked where he lived, Hall said that his home was in Willowbrook near Compton, California. He said he would stay in Hollywood that night to be near his daughter, and obtained Frith's address which he scribbled on the back of an envelope.

The following day Frith hungrily read the details of the wreck and tried to correlate his personal experience with the newspaper stories. His suspicions were immediately aroused upon reading that the veteran engineer and fireman were the only persons injured in the wreck. It became readily apparent to Mr. Frith and his family that Hall and the train robber were one and the same person, and that he fitted published descriptions of the desperado in every detail. They had opened their hearts to a man who supposedly had a seriously injured daughter, only to find they had been innocently duped into aiding and abetting a criminal's escape.

The Burbank Police Department, after hearing about Frith's embarrassing experience, alerted the Los Angeles County Sheriff's office. All points were informed by bulletins which were processed and distributed in an effort to apprehend and remove from circulation a mad man whose viciousness was exceeded only by his daring.

Following up on the robber's coat, evidence was developed indicating that it was made for a man named Armstrong who resided in Pocatello, Idaho, and had the coat finished in Cincinnati, Ohio. It was found upon further investigation that Mr. Armstrong was a respected and well-known resident of the community. Armstrong had sold the coat to a second-hand clothing dealer in May 1929, and it was later found that the cleaning marks were from a Pocatello cleaning firm. Hopes by law officers that Armstrong and Hall were the same individual were soon blasted when it was found that Armstrong was employed by the city of Pocatello, and that he was working on the date of the robbery. The second-hand clothing dealer was then interrogated and he said that he had no record of the sale involving the suspect's coat. It must have been a great discouragement to investigating officers to be led up two blind alleys, but in the best traditions of their service they persisted in the case and their valiant efforts were soon to satisfy justice.

Closer analysis of the desperado's jacket revealed a rather accurate record of its owner. Hair on the coat was subjected to close scrutiny by laboratory experts of the Los Angeles Police Department, who came up with the following information: They deduced that the person who wore the coat was about 40 years of age, with light colored hair which was very dirty. The coat was worn in the proximity of cattle or other stock and probably belonged to a cowboy.

Then, like a bolt from the blue, the first real tangible evidence came to light right in the middle of an unsolvable paradox. A Los Angeles County deputy, who was assigned to the burglary detail, received a tip from attorney E. G. Hewitt who resided in Los Angeles. Hewitt informed Deputy T. J. Higgins that an ex-convict named Tom Vernon was probably responsible for the train wreck and robbery. Vernon, who was paroled from Folsom Prison in August 1929, had been acting as a caretaker at Mr. Hewitt's home. Hewitt ordered Vernon from his property when he found that the parolee had been leaving the residence at night equipped with the attorney's pistol. Vernon proudly displayed his native ingenuity by showing Hewitt a pair of rubber gloves from which he had cut the trigger finger. Before leaving his benefactor's home, Vernon stole some clothing and money, and also absconded with a revolver. The last act was no doubt motivated by a desire to insure an adequate income . . . lawful or mostly otherwise.

Enigmatic as it may seem, Deputy Higgins knew Tom Vernon well, having become acquainted with him because of his activities as an informer. A few years before, Vernon had been a prisoner in the Los Angeles County Jail, and his assistance had aborted an attempted break-out. At the time, Vernon was about 43 years old, and had spent 22 of those in various prisons, evidently becoming expert in committing felonies. His dexterity in this regard assured his repeated entry into the "big house." Vernon had been a six-time loser, and he had been imprisoned in the Pennsylvania and Ohio State prisons, graduating to California's San Quentin prison near fog-shrouded San Francisco Bay just after his western sojourn. The suspect had also served three terms on the rock pile at Folsom, located in the torrid foothills east of Sacramento, California.

As a result of his preliminary investigation,

Higgins obtained a photograph of Vernon, and with his partner approached the officers assigned to the case. The two deputies were put on the Saugus crime by Sheriff Traeger, and he encouraged them to prosecute to finalization. Mixing Vernon's picture with those of other known criminals, the two deputies took them to the Frith family for a show-down. Without any appreciable effort they picked Tom Vernon's photographs from the "mugs" and then positively identified him as the man they had befriended at the service station in Saugus the night of November 10, 1929.

There was no doubt about it. He was definitely the man who had ridden into Los Angeles with them, employing a ruthless guise that took the Friths on a merry-go-round of emotional frustration. Shaken by the experience, they were completely "wrung-out." It was soon established why Vernon was so conversant in matters "cow-wise" . . . when not in prison he worked as a stockman and rodeo performer, no doubt specializing in the legal derailment of genus Bovine!

Following this lead, the deputies took their portable "line-up" to the train crew, and also showed Vernon's photograph to the passengers of the ill-fated train. This proved to "nail" Vernon down as the train robber. Victim after victim identified him as the little desperado with the big "equalizer." Upon examination of further information gathered from informers, etc., Tom Vernon was placed in the Saugus area on the date of the crime.

About two weeks after the Saugus incident, a crack Union Pacific Railroad passenger train hit the ballast near Cheyenne, Wyoming. This wreck happened on November 23, 1929, and as if to fit a well-planned pattern, the passengers were robbed by a lone masked bandit fitting Vernon's basic description. Union Pacific's No. 17 was wrecked in almost the same manner as was the West Coast Limited, and the similiarities of the crimes were amazing. Pressuring themselves to the limit, the law enforcement agencies realized it was extremely urgent that the maniac responsible for these depredations be taken out of circulation permanently. Maximum effort was now exerted in an attempt to capture Vernon before he diverted all of America's crack passenger trains to the ties!

A bizarre aspect of the case developed on about November 23, 1929 when Deputy Higgins, attorney Hewitt, and Hewitt's secretary, Miss Serrano, each received separate letters postmarked in Cheyenne. Vernon, in an apparent attempt to establish an alibi, wrote that he had left Los Angeles by motor truck on the morning of November 10, 1929. His anxieties were well supported, because he knew he was facing a death penalty for train wrecking. He also knew that the web of evidence would soon encompass him, and terminate the heinous activities that he found himself occupied with. His alibi was emphasized in each individual letter and this was no doubt an obvious attempt to establish the fact that he was not in the Saugus area on November 10th.

On the day following the robbery of Union Pacific No. 17, a special session of the Grand Jury for the County of Los Angeles was convened. All information was presented, and the expected result was forthcoming. Tom Vernon was indicted and charged with train wrecking and robbery. His written alibi was soon disproved by locating several witnesses who testified that he had visited persons in Los Angeles on the night of November 10th. It was found that some time after leaving the Friths, he purchased flowers and took them to a Los Angeles hospital. Not for his imaginary daughter, the offering was intended for a lady friend, but the lateness of the hour required that he return the next morning. What manner of woman could motivate this man to commit such a crime? Now, it was positively established that Vernon was not only in the Los Angeles area on November 10th, but he was also there the next day. This blasted his patented cover-up into a million pieces.

The die was cast, and Deputy Higgins rushed to Denver, Colorado in an attempt to apprehend and arrest Vernon. Before going to Cheyenne, Higgins learned that the train wrecker had stayed at the Manx Hotel in the mile high city, and while the deputy interrogated the hotel staff, he came up with the "clincher." A chamber-maid produced a note Vernon had left for her which read: "House-maid, if I can ever help you, write me." As if devoid of all mentality, Vernon signed it "Buffalo Tom Vernon," and conveniently included his address as Pawnee, Oklahoma, in care of Pawnee Bill's Buffalo Ranch. The case was assuming proportions bordering on the ridiculous. But the results of Vernon's ruthlessness were less than amusing to his victims.

Joining forces with Sheriff Romsa of Cheyenne and Special Agent Matt McCourt of the Union Pacific Railroad, Higgins rushed to Pawnee, Oklahoma in an effort to find Vernon. Find him they did on December 1, 1929, and together with Sheriff Alan Jones of Pawnee County, arrested him on the warrant issued for him on the California train wrecking charge. The next day produced the fruitful results for which Higgins had worked so hard. Tom Vernon confessed that he had wrecked Southern Pacific's No. 59 and had also robbed its passengers. But they weren't going to pin the Union

Pacific "rap" on him. He denied all responsibility or that he took any part in the U.P. robbery, and was very adamant in that regard. The sheriff from Cheyenne, along with the Union Pacific's Special Agent, felt that Vernon was lying and knew they had a very strong case against him. In view of the facts and clues they had, they promptly filed a request with the Governor of Oklahoma for Vernon's extradition to Wyoming.

On December 4, 1929, the Los Angeles County Grand Jury returned another indictment, charging Vernon with the Saugus train wreck and four counts of robbery. On that same day, Governor Young of California signed extradition papers which were forwarded by air mail to the Governor of Oklahoma.

A legal tug-of-war seemed to develop as Wyoming officers asked for Vernon's return because they felt they also had a conviction assured. Deputy Higgins wired California Attorney General Webb, requesting all possible assistance in having Vernon returned to California for prosecution. Webb telegraphed the Attorney General of Oklahoma, assuring him of a positive conviction in view of Vernon's confession. Los Angeles County District Attorney Buron Fitts was notified that a hearing was to be convened in the Governor's office at Oklahoma City, Oklahoma on December 7, 1929. Buron Fitts chartered an airplane on December 6th and arrived in time for the important hearing.

The meeting was attended by an imposing array of personalities which included Oklahoma's Governor William J. Holloway and his Attorney Baxter Taylor. Also in attendance were County Attorney Pickett of Cheyenne, Wyoming, Special Agent McCourt of the Union Pacific Railroad, Sheriff Romsa of Cheyenne, District Attorney Fitts and Deputy Higgins from Los Angeles County. All facts and related data concerning the Saugus robbery were outlined. Fitts presented the evidence, which was reaching massive proportions by now, and capped it off with Vernon's confession. He had evidently influenced Sheriff Jones of Pawnee, Oklahoma, because when Jones testified, he stated that he arrested Vernon for the California authorities. He stated that they assumed prior rights to the robber. The Wyoming authorities knew they had been pre-empted, and considering Vernon's confession of the West Coast Limited robbery, felt their case was slipping away from them. Vernon had clung to his original denial of any complicity in the Union Pacific train wrecking in Wyoming.

Governor Holloway concluded the lengthy hearing and his decision called for Deputy Higgins to return Vernon to California for prosecution. Higgins returned the robbery suspect to Los

Angeles by train, arriving on December 9, 1929. Vernon was then put through the "ringer" by Southern Pacific's Chief O'Connell and Captain Brooks of Los Angeles County. After a round of thorough questioning, Vernon made his second complete confession, and was then returned to the scene of the crime. He was asked to show where he tampered with the rails and pointed out the exact spot. Vernon had also showed the officers where he waited in ambush and watched the head-end of the train turn over. His sadistic nature caused him to brag about his attempt to wreck the Owl, but that train luckily negotiated the unspiked rails without incident.

While other legalities of the case were being settled, Higgins followed up on the important coat identified as being worn by Vernon. The indefatigable deputy found that the coat was part of a suit issued to Vernon on his release from Folsom prison in August of 1929. The coat had been purchased from a second-hand clothing dealer in Pocatello, Idaho by a fellow inmate who identified it. It had been added to the prison wardrobe pool, and then issued to Tom Vernon upon his release from the institution. Thus, the deputy's thoroughness helped forge another link in a steel chain of evidence that was designed to permanently restrain a mad-dog train robber.

On December 12, 1929, Tom Vernon appeared before Los Angeles Superior Court Judge Aggeler, and entered a plea of guilty to train wrecking and one count of robbery. He pled not guilty to three additional counts of robbery, and was represented by a Public Defender named Davis. Davis wisely ordered a psychiatric examination of his client because of his prison record, which carried a notation signed by a doctor. It read: syphilitic-cured. Davis felt he could base his defense on the premise that Vernon was insane, and the court promptly appointed three doctors to check Vernon's sanity. On December 17, 1929 the doctors adjudged Vernon sane and mentally responsible for his acts under the meaning of the law. Subsequently Attorney John Cooper acted as counsel for Tom Vernon, but his efforts came to naught. It was widely rumored that the Indian scout, rancher and showman, Major G. W. Lillie, had engaged Cooper in Vernon's defense. Vernon had worked for the old gentleman at one time, and Major Lillie evidently felt that he had to finance the criminal defense for old-time sake.

The police were hindered by a myriad of confessions, and one such admission of guilt was volunteered by Lester Mead. Mead showed up at Los Angeles Police Headquarters just after the Saugus depredation and confessed that he was responsible for the wreck and robbery of the West

Coast Limited. Primarily, it was Mead's ability to read the newspapers, and his contact with sensation seeking news reporters that allowed him to acquire many facts relative to this crime. However, when taken to Saugus to reconstruct the crime, he failed miserably. He was taken to the point where 5042 had hit the ground, and he didn't even know what direction to go to find the tool house. His story was "shot full of holes," and his confession was incomplete and fabricated with far too many discrepancies. His reference to time and distances proved that his sole purpose was to gain false notoriety regardless of the consequences. He was far from the mark and this fact eliminated him as a suspect.

The officers checked his past and found that he and his brother had been inmates of an insane asylum in Washington State. He resumed his residency in a mental institution soon after his confession was completely disproved. Mead had basked in the limelight of publicity, reveling in a joyous psychoneurotic dream world that happily included the real, startling blue-white dazzling flash of photographer's bulbs and the eventual front page news release of sensational impact.

As if to challenge Mead for his position of priority on the front pages of the tabloids, Vernon claimed to be the son of James and "Cattle Kate" Averill, who ended their career while dancing grotesquely at the end of a rope for rustling cattle in Wyoming. Vernon's erratic story, and his idiotic conduct during the commission of the crime, would lead one to think that perhaps he should have been committed to a medical facility. Be that as it may, Vernon's association with cattle and horses should have ended in the rodeo arena. Little did he suspect that during the glamorous heyday of the cowboy shows he would be destined to become the victim of a much wilder horse . . . one of ferrous structure. Southern Pacific's 5042 was the last bronco Tom Vernon would bust and he came out second best for his involvement in this senseless crime.

Time was fast running out for Vernon. On December 18, 1929, sentence was pronounced on the train wrecker by Judge Aggeler. Vernon faced the austere Judge, and took a lifetime sentence without hope of parole. The convicted robber didn't even "bat an eye," and the train wrecker appeared to be standing in an emotional vacuum. Vernon, like so many of his bovine victims, had reached the end of his rope. The State and Federal laws called for execution on the train wrecking charge, and this is exactly what District Attorney Fitts pressed for. However, Vernon was sentenced to Folsom prison for life under provisions of the California Habitual Criminal Act and also five years to life on the robbery charge. He was escorted to Folsom prison, then processed for a life of confinement. The dreary rock quarries of this maximum security installation must have seemed like home to him, and he was certified to his former assignment as a hoist engineer. Considering the many times he was imprisoned, his make-up must have included a hidden desire to be in the "lock-up" at all times. Was the loneliness of the "outside" a driving force that caused Vernon to seek the companionship and security of penal confines? He seemed to be most happy in Folsom, and the officials considered him an excellent prisoner even though he had written several letters claiming that he had been framed.

Nevertheless, Tom Vernon served about 35 years in prison for the Saugus "caper." He was released on parole about 1964. A short time after his parole, Governor Edmund G. Brown gave Vernon his final pardon. Though a writ of Habeas Corpus was presented in Vernon's behalf on May 1947, its denial by the California Supreme Court was to eventually be nullified by the final pardon extended to the old, graying prisoner.

The author would suggest that the *Southern Pacific Class* 5000 steam engines had reason, other than technical, to produce their stuttering exhausts. Considering the weird experiences that were visited upon their herd, little more reason need be cited to explain their strange stack mutterings.

Although Buffalo Tom Vernon was to spend a majority of his life confined behind prison bars, the three-cylinder giants enjoyed the unrestricted expanse of the desolate west, and continued to chuckle away the endless miles. Vernon's imprisonment in no way eased the inherent fear that the huge 4-10-2's became imbued with. Allowing consideration for past experiences, they were to forever continue their stammering talk without criticism. However, their fears were misdirected.

Like all other locomotives powered by steam, the *Southern Pacific* and the *Overland Class* engines were to someday make the final run. Their ultimate demise was finally occasioned by the encroachment of colorfully enameled legions of gaudy "skunks." Provocative as the word PROGRESS may seem in this regard, the Diesel revolution on America's railroads eventually brought superannuation to the steamers. PROGRESS forced the three-cylinder beauties from the high steel to the unwarranted imposition of the dreary locomotive graveyards.

Occasional releases to alleviate seasonal shortages only served to temporarily forestall the inevitable switching movement down the rusty rails to the junkers.

As ashes and dust so return . . . so did the 4-10-2's return to the searing flames of the open hearth furnaces from whence they came.

Born of Flame . . . They Lived of Fire . . .

And So They Died . . .

Lonely and temporarily deserted, the retired SP-1 waits for the biting cut of the scrapper's torch. Photograph taken at Portland, Oregon, July 1954.

Larry Harrison collection.

53

The lost engine of Woodford, California is shown here after her complete rebuilding and subsequent return to service on the Tehachapi Pass railroad. Jerry Best caught her about eight months after the disaster on a sunny afternoon at Bakersfield, California. Looking much like she did when built, the expert rebuilding by the shop crew at San Bernardino, California left no visible evidence of the terrific damages sustained by her fall into Tehachapi Creek. Photograph taken April 9, 1933.

Gerald M. Best photograph.

This was the point engine that powered the Southern Pacific train stalled at Woodford, California during the terrific cloudburst of September 1932. The huge "back-up" Mallie is shown in later years at Los Angeles, California, photographed on March 9, 1946, seven years prior to her scrapping. The placement of the cab was possible only because these engines burned oil fuel. Crude oil in their tenders was kept under slight pressure so that it would flow the length of the long boiler and be available at the burner in full volume.

F. C. Smith photograph.

Guy L. Dunscomb collection.

This AC-5 engine was the second helper cut into second section of No. 818 just 13 cars ahead of the caboose. The big cab-ahead 4-8-8-2 and her sister engine 4110 were untouched by the flood disaster that coursed down the 18 mile Tehachapi Canyon on September 30, 1932. The cab forward design was necessitated by the use of these locomotives in long tunnels and snow sheds. By placing the cab ahead, engine crews were positioned ahead of the stack and were spared the discomfort of breathing hot exhaust gasses and steam. All Southern Pacific 4-8-8-2's were built by Baldwin Locomotive Works between 1928 and 1944. Photograph taken at Los Angeles, California on September 18, 1938.

Allan Youell photograph.

Chapter Three

Cloudburst on Tehachapi

The weather was cloudy late in the afternoon of September 30, 1932. Southern Pacific's 5036 was cut into Second 818 as the swing helper and was trained 29 cars ahead of the caboose. The huge *Southern Pacific Class* engine was one of two helper locomotives cut-in and assisting the point engine 4110 in boosting her 66 loads up over the heavy grades of the Tehachapi Pass in California. Engine 4125 was the other engine, and like the road engine, was a cab-ahead 4-8-8-2. Engineer A. S. Hirst and Fireman C. E. Bloomfield were in charge of 4125, and the big articulated locomotive was trained about 13 cars ahead of the "hack." This liberal accumulation of motive power proved how steep the tortuous grades were on the transit over the 4,025 foot summit to Mojave, California.

As Second 818 picked its way out through the yard tracks at Bakersfield, California and headed east through Kern Junction, Engineer Alexander Ross, who was running the big three barreled engine, commented to his Fireman, Enos Brown, about the unusually heavy concentration of thunderheads piling up over the mountains. As the train rumbled through Bena, raindrops hitting the smokebox of the laboring locomotive exploded into little puff-balls of steam. Both enginemen expressed hope that the huge masses of soft cumulus clouds would bring relief to the parched foothills in the form of a cooling shower.

That word shower could hardly have been less appropriate, as the towering pink clouds catching the afternoon sun at their crests were soon to precipitate one of the most devastating flash floods on the hill since Bill Hood engineered the railroad in 1876. With smoke and steam flying, 5036 chanted to the increase of the ascending grade, and the reaction at the stack was an audible indication that Ross had "dropped 'er down." Brown got off his seatbox and moved Brakeman Harry Moore from the top of the steel box-like sand container which was mounted on the cab

end of the tender. Lifting the heavy metal lid, Brown found the scoop and drove it into the abrasive, filling it to the brim.

With a swift motion, Brown stepped over the steel apron that separated the engine cab from the tender, lifted the peephole on the fire-door, and placed the scoop at the glaring white-hot hole. The vacuum sucked the sand from the scoop, and the engine's exhaust became a muffled roar as the soot and carbon scoured from the clogged flues filled the smokebox and choked off the stack. The insulating carbon shot from the smokestack in a high graceful black plume. The fireman repeated the process until he was sure the fire-tubes were blasted clean. The steam pressure needle on his gauge reacted instantly and steadily climbed to maximum as Enos readied the pounding 4-10-2 for the heavy work ahead.

Climbing back on his seatbox on the left side of the ponderous three-holer, Brown poked his head out the window for a cool breath of air and then turned his attention to the warm interior of the cab, checking the water glass along with the conglomeration of valves on the firing manifold. A comfortable sense of well-being consumed the crew of the free steaming locomotive, and they knew that everything was under control. They luxuriated in this knowledge as they watched the darkening storm condense over the Tehachapi Mountains. They marvelled at the intensity of the startling electrical activity surrounding 6,900 foot Bear Mountain and were greatly impressed as they watched nature's fireworks dance along the 7,500 foot crest of Breckenridge to the north. These two peaks were part of the western watershed of the Tehachapi Range that drained through the narrow rocky gorges cut by Caliente and Tehachapi Creeks.

By now word had filtered through the telegraph that this violent storm was a killer, and that it had broken over the summit with a wall of water that was descending on the desert divide. Rumors came clicking into Woodford depot, with some excited reports telling that the little mountain railroad station at Tehachapi Pass was destroyed by the deluge. Section men reported that the rising streams were posing a threat to the tracks that followed the twisting contours of the foothill canyons. Then more startling news came into the Woodford depot in the form of excited dots and dashes as Frank Nejedly, the swing shift operator, heard the incredulous message stating that the cement plant at Monolith had been heavily damaged by the storm waters.

Reports came fast now. Track walkers informed officials that the railroad embankments were starting to crumble and fall into the roaring waters. The water mad stream was rising at an incredible rate. It was decided that any eastbound trains should be side tracked at Woodford for their own protection. The dispatcher headed First 818, a Santa Fe freight train, into Woodford siding. This train, with 40 loads under the charge of Conductor J. Mulvana, pulled up the long siding to the east end and stopped in the clear of the mainline. When First 818 came to a stop, the helper engine 3834, a big boilered 2-10-2, was spotted on the rim above the roaring creek about 100 feet east of Woodford depot.

It was raining harder than ever now. The crew from the helper engine dashed to the yellowed station, but were thoroughly drenched by the time they reached their refuge. Nejedly sat statue-like in the bay window listening to the incredible reports that flooded from his telegraph key. The old wooden depot was musty and drab, but the pot bellied stove, now bulging with coal, gave a warm penetrating glow. The excited trainmen gathered around the "bug" listening to Nejedly as he deciphered the code messages. Frank had the word now. Second 818 would head-in at Woodford and pull up behind the Santa Fe train because the railroad fills were disintegrating along the tight defiles of the normally dry creek. This was Southern Pacific track, but was jointly used by Santa Fe trains through Tehachapi Pass to Mojave, California where the "iron cross" took off on its own roadbed and headed east across the arid desert to Barstow, California.

Woodford at milepost 248.8 was only about ten miles west of the summit and had yet to feel the brunt of the terrible storm. Little did Nejedly and the small group of railroad men know, but the stage was irrevocably set for one of the most fantastic disasters ever recorded in the annals of western railroading.

As increasing masses of tortured, fulminating clouds writhed and twisted up into the stratosphere, streaks of brilliant blue lightning pulled ominous sheets of water from their undersides. Woodford was now coming in for its share of the storm as Second 818 reached the west switch of the passing track, and Engineer E. Bishop on 4110 eased her into the water-soaked siding. C. R. Thompson was boiling water for Bishop on the big articulated engine. Their manifest consisted of perishables and live stock destined for the eastern markets. The familiar smell of wet sagebrush invaded the closed cab, but went unheeded, although it was a wind-driven warning of things to come.

The horrible storm lashed at Woodford with unabated fury. The cyclonic turbulence created by the intensifying magnitude of the winds began tearing branches off the scraggly oaks. Tufts of brown grass swirled into the air as if the whirlwinds were obliged to strip the softly contoured hills of all vegetation. The thunderous roar that followed a garish flash of lightning soon brought a torrent of solid water from the tormented sky. The storm was then smothering the little mountain depot and her nestling trains in a blanket of rain so intense that it even caused rivulets of water to move against the force of gravity. Nearly 2,709 feet up on the side of Tehachapi Range, Woodford station and the trains in her protective custody stood alone, bracing against the most powerful onslaught nature could extract from her bag of tricks.

As Second 818 closed up onto the Santa Fe caboose, the surrounding hills became livid under the nightmarish glare of the increasing electrical discharges. The inky blackness of the sky produced an eerie backdrop to an unbelievable scene as the bolts of lightning unveiled a macabre view of a solid world suddenly gone fluid.

When Second 818 made her final stop, 5036, by some unaccountable quirk of fate, was left spotted on a huge concrete culvert spanning Tehachapi Creek. The culvert brought the main and siding track from the north bank of the dusty creek to the south side to avoid a jutting ridge in the mountains.

After the Southern Pacific train stopped, Pinkey Ross told Enos Brown that he was going over to a nearby restaurant for a hamburger and cup of coffee. Brown chose to stay with his three-cylinder brute; a decision that had definite influence on his longevity.

Setting a low spot fire in 5036's firebox, Enos closed his cab window to the raging storm, stretched his legs out and put his feet up on the warm boiler-head. Slipping into a slicker and pulling his cap down over his head, the 50 year-old engineer slid down the grab-irons and disappeared into the deluge as he headed for the little cafe built on the bank of Tehachapi Creek.

From his vantage point high on the concrete bridge over the rising waters of the violent stream, Brown idly speculated on how long their freight train would be tied up at the isolated station. He called Moore's attention to the many forms of debris that were floating down the swirling stream, and they watched in amazement as the water backed up behind the culvert. The floating crest provided a moving kaleidoscope of thick soupy browns and blacks as the churning waters eddied against the bridge. The rapidly rising waters were glutted with tree trunks, roots and branches and the roar of the creek was soon audible above the crashing thunder.

Although designed and built to handle a large volume of runoff water, the concrete bridge soon became a dam, and its ability to disgorge itself of the flood waters and debris became questionable. Brakeman Moore told Brown he didn't believe they should stay, and immediately displayed his anxiety by crossing from one side of the gangway to the other checking the flow of the racing flood waters. Brown watched the show from his high perch, completely astonished by the rate of rising flood tide, and he seemed transfixed by a dreamlike immobility that negated all attempts to escape from his predicament. Even as the spectre of falling into a watery grave grew more imminent by the second, Brown couldn't seem to overcome the numbness to forestall his pending doom. Before he could leave the big 4-10-2 and gain the advantage of high ground, a flood surge brought the crest of foaming water up and over the rails, and in an instant half way to the cab of the 5036. The fireman then knew that it would be suicide to attempt to leave the big engine, and he knew that they would all share the same fate in the swirling waters. The ungodly roar of the rushing waters was now deafening. Brown found it hard to believe his eyes when the churning currents started cutting the embankments from both ends of the culvert, isolating the big locomotive in the middle of the rising flood.

The fireman snapped back to reality. The distraction of the storm that held him spellbound was broken when Moore said he was going over the top in an attempt to reach the safety of the caboose. Sadly, it was the last time the brakeman was seen alive.

The time was about 8:15 P.M. and the storm had reached its deadly climax, tearing at the railroad with unbridled ferocity. Moore lit his lantern and climbed out of the sheltering cab, cautiously crossing the top of the slippery Vanderbilt tender. Leaning into the strong wind, Moore crossed to the first car behind the stranded helper engine.

Without warning, the flood crest suddenly swelled up to nearly 50 feet, tumbling Moore and the five cars that were immediately behind the helper engine into the raging torrent. Moore's pitiful screams for help were for naught with the noise of the crashing waters drowning out his final call for help as he was swallowed by the silted flood waters. Brown watched in horror as a boxcar was washed from the front of the 5036 and rolled onto its side at the base of the bridge.

The waters extinguished the fire in the SP-2's boiler, and were then running through the cab deck between the engine and tender. It was at about this time that the fireman sensed a feeling he had never before experienced. As the flood passed over the culvert, the ballast and rip-rap that back-filled the structure was washing out and undermining the locomotive. The heavy steamer rolled to her right, and then settled into the water with a sickening surge, scraping the engineer's side of the boiler against the south abutment. The tender and cab end of the boiler dropped into the depression with her stack and boiler front assuming a higher position.

When the locomotive settled, the fireman scrambled along the running board to the front end of the boiler. Brown was soaked to the skin. His position on the highest part of the engine was fast becoming untenable as the water kept coming up from the bowels of the crazy creek. Clinging to the clam-shell deflector-type smoke stack, the plucky fireman hung on for dear life as the strong currents tore at his body, attempting to wrest him from his island of steel. Brown's prayers were certainly answered. The request for a parole from the grasping fingers of Tehachapi Creek was soon forthcoming when the flood waters leveled off and started to ebb. The receding waters disclosed that the 5036 had finally come to rest, turning nearly 90 degrees from her original attitude, her eventual release dictated by the whims of the tremendous storm.

Meanwhile, when Alexander Ross arrived at the Bear Mountain service station and restaurant close to the banks of the rocky creek, the door swung open to admit him into the smoky interior. Ross was relieved when the closing door shut out the sound of the mad waters. Peter Kaad and his wife Louise were the operators of the cafe, and they were busily preparing hot cakes and coffee for a group of about 20 transients who had left the stalled freight train to seek a haven from the drenching cloudburst. The restaurant had taken on a festive air as Mr. Kaad's son played his violin in defiance of the noisy downpour outside.

Just how many people were gathered in the little one room cafe will never be known because most of them were transients, including two 18 year old girls dressed in overalls. As Peter Kaad Jr. broke into "River Stay Way From My Door," a Southern Pacific section foreman named Nick Tom entered the cafe and informed its occupants that they had better evacuate the premises for safety's sake. Kaad Sr. looked at the mud soaked track worker and informed him that he had been through many storms before, and that this particular one didn't seem to be any worse than the others.

As if completely oblivious of the storm, the little party continued despite the destruction being wrought along the 20 mile canyon of death. Again Nick shoved his way into the crowded eatery, pleading with them to seek higher ground, but his professional evaluation, based on years of experience, went unnoticed. The nice warm cafe, smelling of hot cakes and aromatic coffee, held the little group like a magnet as the storm brewed outside with frightful violence. None of the people in the restaurant desired to leave, the palate-tickling smell of cooking hamburger mixed with the tantalizing odor of sweet frying onions permeated the room, causing a paralysis in the lower extremities.

Peter Jr.'s musical admonition, designed to stay the waters of the creek, was without result as water was seen rising through the floor of the building. Kaad Sr. reassured the little crowd that he had been through several storms worse than this, and that he had also experienced several floods. His statements pacified the people who felt that perhaps Kaad was some sort of expert on this type of thing, and their fears continued to be allayed. Kaad stated that his service station was safe, and that Nick Tom was inclined toward excitability without good reason. He had no sooner uttered his indictment of the section foreman when the electricity failed, plunging the startled group into darkness. Mrs. Kaad promptly lit an antique kerosene lantern held in reserve for such emergencies, and hung it from a nail driven in a beam above the counter. Water was shoe-top high now, and the restaurant owner's wife started to move her supply of foodstuffs to higher shelves along the dingy wall. As the people nervously joked about the rain and rising water, Mr. Tom made his third and final appeal. As he was rebuffed, Peter Jr. sawed away on his violin, changing his tune to "It Ain't Gonna Rain No More No More." But rain it did, and the deluge fell in solid sheets much more voluminous than the proverbial cascade of "cats and dogs."

E. A. Beuer, a transient from the stalled train, was part of the group of people in the cafe, along with F. B. Shalliar of San Francisco, Cali-fornia. They had expressed concern about the rising flood and were about to leave when the world came apart. One wall of the building was blasted into the interior of the room with an explosive force by a huge wave of flood water. The building shuddered and then disintegrated into a swirling vortex of rubble. The flotsam from the splintered restaurant, along with its occupants, was swept into the swollen creek, and the shrieks of the victims could be heard above the howling winds. Shalliar had fought his way toward the back door of the cafe, but the door soon came to him instead. After what seemed like hours, he surfaced and found that he was being swept downstream. Feeling as if he had swallowed half the water of the muddy stream, Shalliar luckily grabbed the top of a tree and held on for what seemed an interminable period of time. He watched help-lessly as Mrs. Kaad's body swept by on the roaring crest surrounded by the lumber that once formed the service station. He noticed several bodies in the surging flood waters, but his involvement with survival prevented him from helping the other victims.

When the storm had subsided and the waters had lowered, rescue units were organized at Bakersfield and rushed to the scene of the disaster. Communications had been severely affected by the waters, and the world knew little of the suffering and death that filled the remote canyon. Nothing remained of the little restaurant except a metal sign which, by some twist of ironic fate, was left standing upright against a tree, inviting those so inclined to "STOP HERE FOR RE-FRESHMENTS." The advertisement was false. The shattered remains of the Kaad restaurant had sped seaward along with the bodies of those who were not fortunate enough to free themselves from the wreckage.

Of the five locomotives held at Woodford, Santa Fe 3834 proved to be in the most disadvan-tageous position. The vicious currents of water deflected from the rocks on the north bank of the creek formed extreme turbulence just under the point at which the Santa Fe helper locomotive had stopped. Rocks and soil boiled from under the heavy 2-10-2 until there was no support for the big engine spotted on the rim above the roiling canyon stream. Hidden by a blinding veil of rain, the locomotive rolled into the bank-full creek without allowing the awesome spectacle to be witnessed by human eyes.

When the storm had finally slackened its fury, interested persons went seeking out their locomotive. The engineer and fireman from Santa Fe 3834 stared wide-eyed at the void that was once occupied by their 200-ton locomotive. The

Aerial view taken the day after the flood disaster showing final resting place of the helper engine. The big 4-10-2 is shown lying against the south abutment of the huge culvert and the vicious waters have left only the largest of boulders, washing other fill downstream. Mainline and other auxiliary tracks have been deflected by the terrific flood torrent that was dammed by the tree gutted culvert.

Scene about 100 feet east of Woodford station shows where Santa Fe helper engine slid into creek. Engine 3834 was cut into First No. 818 just ahead of the Santa Fe refrigerator car shown at right in the photograph. This scene greeted the engine crew when they went looking for their engine, and much to their amazement they could not locate their charge. Impossible as it may seem, the heavy 2-10-2 was found downstream about 150 feet below the obvious point where she stood on long siding. Her boiler front was found nearly opposite the rear of the "reefer" shown in the picture. The water pressures necessary to deflect a 200 ton locomotive this distance staggers the imagination.

Guy L. Dunscomb collection.

Wearing a shroud of mud and sand, the big Santa Fe type engine lies in her burial vault located under nearly ten feet of alluvium deposited on her by the raging currents of the water crazed creek. This picture taken during the early part of October 1932, shows the seepage that has encroached upon the first excavation work. The locomotive faces upstream toward the right which was in the direction of Tehachapi Summit.

Guy L. Dunscomb collection.

Southern Pacific bridge is shown spanning a dry wash that was recently bank full of flood water. A box car can barely be seen against steel viaduct supports at right side of photograph. Photograph was taken in the vicinity of Rowen station near milepost 345.

Guy L. Dunscomb collection.

Washed out Southern Pacific track is suspended over concrete culvert that failed to handle flood waters. The little bridge was supposed to bring the waters under the high fill, but could not capacitate the terrific run-off. Dammed up flood waters soon raged over the top of the embankment, cutting it away and completely destroyed the mainline track. Photograph taken near Caliente, California on October 3, 1932.

Guy L. Dunscomb collection.

This scene taken between Woodford and Caliente shows terrible flood damage inflicted on Southern Pacific tracks by a cloudburst on Tehachapi Range. The storm reached its peak about 8 p.m., September 30, 1932 and caused an estimated million and one-half dollars in damages to the San Joaquin Division. Displaced track and disjointed rails are in evidence everywhere and the right-of-way that coursed along the right rim of the canyon is completely obliterated. Notice that one section of track has been washed to far side of creek that has ebbed to a mere trickle.

Guy L. Dunscomb collection.

sinking feeling in the pit of their stomachs was certainly justified as they gingerly stepped to the brink of the canyon to look for their engine, and soon found that it was nowhere to be seen. Even after the flood waters had disappeared, the dry creek bottom gave no hint as to the location of the huge locomotive. All that greeted their eyes was a short section of torn siding track which was dangling over the abyss. The water and crude oil compartments of the tender were the only parts of the locomotive found at this time. They had broken loose from the tender-bed and had floated some 250 yards downstream before coming to rest.

When the silt and sand of the stream bottom firmed up a bit, railroaders tramped the drying sands speculating on 3834's final resting place. Buried metal detectors were not available at this time, so an enterprising individual requisitioned a compass from Bakersfield High School. The compass was carried along the drying sands, and at a point about 100 feet from the tracks, the needle showed signs of agitation. The unscientific decision was then made that this was the probable burial site of the Santa Fe engine. An exploratory shaft was sunk at a location directly below where the big helper engine stood on the canyon wall. Although this was the obvious place to dig for the heavy engine, it could not be found at this location. After the employment of more sophisticated equipment, the hidden treasure was finally uncovered. Incredibly, the 200 ton helper engine was washed downstream nearly 150 feet from a location directly below the siding on which she stood. Tehachapi Creek had spirited the big 2-10-2 away from the railroad, and in a fit of frustration covered her with ten feet of silt and boulders in an obvious attempt to hide the crime.

In early October came one of the most dramatic and masterful jobs of locomotive recovery ever witnessed. A private contractor moved onto the creek bottom with his clam-shell equipped crane, and proceeded to excavate the helper engine. Water kept seeping into the pit surrounding the helpless locomotive and a gasoline driven pump was employed around-the-clock in an attempt to dry the site. A spur was then built into the creek bottom from the mainline, and a 200 ton wrecking derrick was moved to the east end of the Santa Fe helper. Once in position, the track was removed and the spur was realigned so that a 250 ton locomotive crane could be spotted at the firebox end of the half buried 2-10-2. A wooden platform was then placed on the south side of 3834 as the clam-shell crane continued to remove the silt and sand from around the mudcaked locomotive. After nearly a month of preparation, the wrecker foreman was ready for his first lift on the locomotive. He

wisely clamped sections of rail to the big engine's wheels, thus eliminating the necessity of setting the engine on track after the lift. A repeat performance of the disastrous flood of a month previous certainly would have caught Santa Fe with their rails down. But then again, these terrible torrents probably occur once in a lifetime. However, had there been a second flood that season, the imposing array of recovery equipment on the creek bottom would certainly have been trapped and buried much like the locomotive it was employed to rescue.

On October 31, 1932, the combined effort of the two locomotive cranes was used to raise the crippled engine onto the prepared platform. The damage to the left side of 3834 was almost unbelievable. The cab had been torn from the boiler and most of the jacket and lagging was ripped away. The waters had washed away the cylinder-head covers and divested the big Santa Fe 2-10-2 of most of her appurtenances. The tender-bed and trucks were uncovered just west of the locomotive and were found upside down in the alluvium that tightly gripped the engine. As each shovel full of sand was removed from the 2-10-2, the tremendous damage to the helper engine became more evident.

Santa Fe 3834 became the star in a scenario staged in the amphitheater-like atmosphere of the stream bed. A myriad of spectators lined the rim of the canyon watching a scene much more spectacular than the most epic fictional endeavor. Mother Nature had again upstaged the feeble attempts of man and dazzled an amazed audience with an incredible picture of destruction.

It took exactly one month to recover the 3834 as the powerful derricks gently placed her onto the specially laid cribbing. The big 2-10-2 was finally righted and drawn back to the mainline she knew so well. The bearing surfaces of the silt encrusted locomotive were so badly fouled that it was necessary to pull her out of the stream bed by using the crane's huge powerful hook. The helper engine was then towed to San Bernardino, California where she was completely rebuilt during the next six months. The rails were again laid to the 200 ton derrick that had been spurred east of 3834, and all of the recovery equipment was soon removed from the creek bottom.

Southern Pacific 5036 was recovered in much the same manner as was the Santa Fe helper engine. The track was built from the siding, down along the dry creek bed to the concrete culvert, and the huge three-cylinder engine was rescued. She was then laboriously taken down to a level position by employment of powerful jacks and specially placed wooden blocking. The boulders and rip-rap

Partially uncovered helper engine is shown in early October 1932 after her fall into the mad flood waters of Tehachapi Creek. The boiler has been half uncovered and workmen stand at firebox end of the loco-motive. Exposed tender truck is seen upside down just to rear of locomotive in a pit full of muddy water. The locomotive's bell, num-ber standard and various other parts are still buried beneath the sands of the mountain creek near Wood-ford siding.

Courtesy Sam Zachery.

Sagging steel girder bridge has been hard hit by cresting flood waters. Debris has accumulated against the steel bridge piers and the pressures of the rushing tor-rent has caused partial collapse of the bridge supports. Nearly a dozen bridges were damaged or washed away between Walong and Caliente by the terrific wall of water. Photo-graph taken October 3, 1932.

Guy L. Dunscomb collection.

Initial excavation work in the early part of October, 1932 uncovered the uppermost portion of the engine's boiler here shown resting on its left side at the bottom of Tehachapi Creek. Notice the portable rig used to pump seepage from the rescue scene. This view, taken looking westward along the normally dry creek bottom, looks downstream toward concrete culvert on which Southern Pacific helper engine 5036 stood. Tank portions of Santa Fe 3834's tender floated away on the flood crest and were found several hundred yards downstream.

Courtesy Paul Herbst.

were removed from under the heavy 4-10-2 until she finally assumed a position parallel with the bottom of Tehachapi Creek. She was then pulled back to the railroad by block and tackle manipulated by a Caterpillar of questionable age and ancestry. The right side of the three-cylinder helper engine was badly damaged by contact with the giant boulders on the south abutment. The fireman's side of the locomotive was virtually undamaged, but the cab had been crushed upward by rolling against the side of the gigantic concrete crossing. Damages inflicted on 5036 totaled $9000, plus a sizeable price tag for recovery from the grasp of the massive reinforced concrete culvert. Unbelievably, the headlight and its lens which was mounted on the smokebox door remained unbroken during events that would normally have shattered steel or nerves made of the same material.

A temporary bridge was soon built across the main line side of the culvert, and back filling with rip-rap and earth progressed in a hurried attempt to restore traffic over the summit.

Both 5036 and 3834 were returned to helper service after they were completely rebuilt, and while boosting trains over Tehachapi Pass, they passed the scene of their former embarrassment without a hitch. Santa Fe 3834 remained in helper service until the very end of steam on the hill, passing Woodford depot many times in a dignified manner.

Details of the first few days of rescue were lacking because of heavy damage to the pole lines and the large deposits of mud that were found on the highway that wound through the Pass. The following account of the storm appeared in the Los Angeles Herald Express the next day:

Los Angeles, California
October 1, 1932

CANYONS OF TEHACHAPI SWEPT BY STORM

Thirty lives were estimated to have been lost in the cloudburst in Tehachapi Pass. Inspector W. E. Snell of the State Highway Patrol reported to the patrol offices here. Raging flood waters from a terrific cloudburst in Tehachapi Mountains today had taken a toll of 12 reported dead with at least 60 missing, and tremendous property damage, according to reports filtering to the outside world over crippled telegraph wires.

A wall of water 40 feet high swept down the narrow canyon of Tehachapi Pass demolishing the Southern Pacific station at Tehachapi, a gasoline station at Woodford occupied by nearly a score of persons, crashing a locomotive and six freight cars into the canyon depth and tearing out great sections of railroad tracks and highways.

REPORTED DROWNED

Among those reported drowned were, A. H. Ross, Southern Pacific engineer, Mr. & Mrs. Peter Kaad of Woodford, owners of the service station, and their two children. Mrs. Nell Cooper, Caliente telephone operator, and her two year old niece. Two unidentified men believed to be transients. Three patients of the Kern County Tuberculosis Hospital at Keene. Among those reported missing and for whom rescue crews were searching were 20 members of a highway maintenance crew, 13 persons who had taken refuge in Kaad's service station before it was swept away and an unknown number of transients who were said to be riding the freight train. Trainmen said that at least 60 of these transients had been aboard the train.

Southern Pacific tracks and bridges were washed away in half a dozen places. Trains of this road and the Santa Fe which uses the Southern Pacific tracks were re-routed over Coast Lines until the rails can be repaired. Rescue crews from Bakersfield fought their way into the flood region in an effort to locate missing persons and recover bodies.

Two of the bodies were found near Woodford. One was identified as Peter Kaad, 19, and the other remained unidentified. The wreck of the Southern Pacific freight train was a sudden and terrifying spectacle according to Enos A. Brown, fireman who battled his way to safety out of the roaring waters. The train was standing on a siding partly on a trestle beneath which the swirling flood was rapidly rising.

The torrent tore against the bank, undermining the roadbed and toppling the locomotive and six cars into the stream. The Kaad service station in which 13 persons were reported to have sought refuge from the drenching rain was hurled into the canyon by the wall of water.

News of Ross' death prostrated his widow. As the Southern Pacific offices here gathered reports from crews in the field, it was learned all bridges on the rail line between Caliente and Bena had been swept away. One bridge was hurled 300 feet downstream. At another place the flood waters hurled more than 1,000 feet of ties and rails from the roadbed into an adjacent cornfield. In addition to the deaths the flood caused large property damage. Highways and railway tracks were torn up, the Southern Pacific station at Tehachapi was destroyed and houses and mountain cabins were swept away.

In the wake of the storm, Tehachapi was virtually isolated by the destruction of telephone and telegraph lines, and it was impossible to verify reports of deaths and damage. Caliente, another small town in the vicinity was under two feet of water in places it was reported. The town of Keene was also flooded but the nearby Tuberculosis Sanitarium of Kern County escaped.

After being blocked by washouts and huge masses of mud which the torrent deposited along the pavement, the highway through Tehachapi Pass was opened to light traffic today. The road between Oak Glen and Camp Tejon was closed by a rock slide. While only light showers were falling elsewhere in the southland, the mountain cloudburst was said to have registered 4½ inches of rain within a few hours.

Los Angeles Herald Express
Monday, October 3, 1932
HUNT BODIES OF MISSING IN FLOOD

Bodies of 11 persons including two women drowned in the cloudburst which devastated Tehachapi Pass lay in Bakersfield morgues today bringing the known dead to 16. Meanwhile more than 1,000 workers dug in the tangled debris and under banks of silt for the bodies of more than a score of missing believed to have perished. Two pretty young women who were with a large number of transients on a Southern Pacific freight train which was hurled to destruction by a 40' wall of water were among the missing. The only bodies identified were those of Mr. & Mrs. Peter Kaad owners of a service station at Woodford and Mrs. Nell Cooper a Southern Pacific operator at Caliente. The other seven were believed to be itinerants; victims of the wreck of the train. These may later be identified.

THE MISSING

Missing persons include, A. H. Ross, engineer; Harry Moore, brakeman; Annella Williams 2 year old granddaughter of Mrs. Cooper, Clifford Barron of Bellingham, Wash.; and John Tempest of Caliente. Because nearly a dozen autos were found smashed by the flood on a wrecked section of the Tehachapi to Bena highway and because of an unascertained number of transients trapped by a 50 foot wall of floodwater at Woodford-Keene, some estimates placed the number of missing as high as 40. More than a thousand men started rebuilding the 31 miles of Southern Pacific double-track and 16 bridges which were carried away. Damage to the railroad was estimated at $1,500,000 while another $5,000,-000 may represent other material damage in the district.

BODY FOUND

Mrs. Kaad's body was washed 18 miles down-

stream. Bodies of Kaad and his son were found near the site of the garage. Fear was expressed for the safety of Gustave H. Offerman, a teacher of the Tehachapi High School and graduate of the University of Southern California and of Stanford University and Offerman's wife and infant son. Mrs. C. H. Offerman, mother of the teacher said at San Francisco that she had been unable to obtain any word of them. An ironic twist was given to the disaster when prospectors, some of them driving pack laden burros began entering the district. Whenever there is a flood there is usually gold one of the bearded prospectors said. As the plainsmen sought torn banks of soil to delve for wealth, rescue crews were digging for a more gruesome reward — the mangled bodies of the dead. Extent of the damage at Caliente still was unknown because of disrupted communication lines which slowly were being restored today. Telephone service was resumed to Tehachapi from the south with one line in order.

So intense was the downpour that a lake one mile long and ½ mile wide formed six miles south of Mojave. The surface was thick with floating debris A full month will be required to repair the railroad tracks, many sections of which were washed out. No trace yet has been found of a 105 thousand pound [200 ton]* Santa Fe locomotive which was struck by the torrent. The Southern Pacific engine was found partially covered by mud and rocks. First problem of the railroad is to open a temporary single track after which the double track roadbed will be restored. Meanwhile traffic was routed over the Southern Pacific Coast Route.

Out of the confusion of newspaper reports one thing became very evident; Tehachapi Pass was certainly the focal point of the intense storm. While most of the southern part of California had minor showers, a devastating concentration of rain fell on this rather remote section of the mountains. The only other account recorded in the newspapers, attributing injury or death to the storm, occurred at Lancaster, California. A local rancher was riding his horse when a bolt of lightning hit a metal band on his hat killing him and his horse instantly. His gun was melted by the high potential discharge, but none of the bullets had fired. Details of the flood and subsequent rescue efforts were slow in coming out of the canyon, but October 4, 1932 brought the following story from the Los Angeles Herald Express.

DEATH CAR IS HUNTED IN FLOOD

With ten bodies recovered from the debris of

Author's Note.

the cloudburst in Tehachapi Pass and the list of known dead definitely set at 15, searchers in the 20 mile long canyon between Tehachapi and the floor of the San Joaquin Valley today sought a box car buried out of sight in mud and thought to contain 21 additional victims, itinerants who were trapped by a 50 foot wall of flood water.

The revised estimate of total dead today stood at 45 with two million dollars as the estimate of property damage according to Southern Pacific Railway and official Kern County sources.

FIND MORE BODIES

The additional bodies recovered were those of Harry Moore, railroad brakeman and an unidentified trainman. In the Bakersfield morgue were the bodies of Mr. & Mrs. Peter Kaad, their son Peter Jr., Mrs. Nell Cooper, Caliente; Clifford Barron, Bellingham, Wash.; Jerome Baker, San Diego; Harry Moore, Los Angeles; Frederick Kessler, Milwaukee, Wisc.; Thomas Moore, Los Angeles and an unidentified man. Coroner N. C. Houze of Kern County was arranging for an inquest.

Early reports that the flood sweeping down the Pass had destroyed a cement plant belonging to the Monolith Cement Company were later found to be untrue.

The plant was only damaged by loss of $240 worth of equipment and was again in operation according to company officials.

REPAIR TRACKS

While 1,000 men toiled to repair 31 miles of Southern Pacific track which was washed out and replace 19 bridges and trestles on the railway, another 100 searchers worked under State Highway Patrolmen and Kern County Deputy Sheriffs in the search for bodies.

Reports that two young girls, who had been riding as transients dressed in overalls were among those drowned could not be confirmed at Bakersfield where search activities were centered.

The State Highway Department at Sacramento, California announced that repairs were being speeded on highways in the Friday night cloudburst.

The unknown factor of just how many transients were involved in the flood will probably never be known. The uncertainties injected into this horrible disaster can only lead one to speculate on the number of victims lying in unknown and unmarked graves along the course of the canyon stream. One statement found in a newspaper account of the tragedy, coming from a victim in a Bakersfield hospital, inserts a note of conjecture as to how many people were actually involved. "About 25 of us were riding on a car loaded with lumber just behind the engine when the train suddenly stopped at Woodford."

One thing is very clear and can be reported with substantiation: Woodford depot is forever gone, as are the two ill-fated locomotives. However, it is a sure bet that they will be long remembered for the part they played in this incredible story. It is also fair to assume that there are many souvenirs still buried beneath the dry sands of Tehachapi Creek along the narrow borders of the lonely canyon. Somewhere just west of milepost 249 is a buried locomotive bell, as well as other parts of Santa Fe 3834 that were never recovered from the silted deposits along the rock scoured creek bottom.

Will some future generation find these artifacts and wonder about their origin? They will perhaps never know about that terrible night of September 30, 1932 when nature's rampaging spirit held Tehachapi and the mountain railroad in her fickle grasp and forever crushed the future from the bodies of her own children.

Robert E. Searle collection.

THREE BARRELS OF STEAM

After the lost locomotive was located (under 10 feet of sand), a clam-shell crane was moved onto the creek bottom and started the initial excavation work. A portion of the buried engine boiler can be seen in this picture taken early in October 1932. Seepage was a problem that plagued the workmen and a pump was employed around the clock in an effort to dry the rescue scene. Disposal of dirt and rocks posed a big problem because of the limited space at the bottom of the canyon.

Courtesy Sam Zachery.

Stricken locomotive has been partially uncovered by a private contractor, and a spur built between the engine and the mainline. This view looks upstream — showing the terrific erosive effect of the rushing waters. The tender frame and bed along with one truck are shown in foreground, but tank portions floated off and were found downstream. Cab has been torn from locomotive.

James E. Boynton collection.

Oil and water compartments of 3834's tender appear as a dark object among trees directly above locomotive. Woodford, California, early October 1932.

Courtesy Sam Zachery

Partially recovered helper engine is viewed after her release from a ten foot blanket of mud and rock. Hard to imagine is the fact that the flood crest filled this gorge and lapped at the ties of Woodford's long siding track.

Notice sand and rock inside the open smokebox and that various parts of the engine have been removed by means of a cutting torch. Photograph taken in October 1932. Courtesy Sam Zachery.

View shows upper right side of Santa Fe 3834 as seen from the cabless end looking upstream easterly. Isolated 200 ton derrick is outrigged and steadied by all manner of blocking (wedges) awaiting orders for the first lift. The engine tumbled into the canyon from upper right side of photograph.

Paul Herbst.

This photograph taken on October 29, 1932 shows the new spur that was built to allow the 250-ton derrick to approach 3834 from a more advantageous position for a lift on the firebox end of the locomotive. The 200-ton crane is at left rear of photo and private contractor's clam-shell rig powered by a primitive gasoline engine labors to uncover engine.

James E. Boynton collection.

200 ton wrecker has been deployed and temporary spur has been removed allowing the clam-shell to complete the excavation of the lost locomotive of Tehachapi. Skeletonized track above the wrecker boom marks the crest of the roaring waters that filled the normally dry gorge.

Engine has been completely excavated and work has progressed far enough to allow riggers to place cables for initial lift. A portable pump was used in the never ending fight to rid the scene of seepage even though other portions of the creekbed were dry as dust. Spectators line the north bank of the creek and workmen have finished clamping rails to the wheels of the big helper engine.

James E. Boynton collection.

The big moment arrives as the two "big hooks" combine to lift the recently buried engine. The Santa Fe wrecker on the right was spurred out east of the big helper engine, and the tracks were then removed, isolating her with the engine she was to help lift. After being righted, 3834 was drawn out of the canyon depths by the derrick shown at the left. Photograph taken on December 29, 1932.

Guy L. Dunscomb collection.

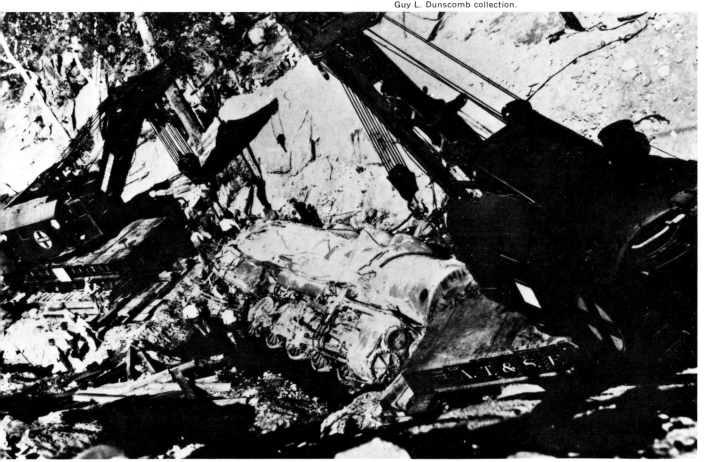

Derrick engineer examines cable placement at front end of engine which hangs in suspension between the two big wrecking derricks. The 200-ton locomotive was lifted onto a special bed layed on the soft silt of the creek bottom.

Guy L. Dunscomb collection.

The lost locomotive of Woodford is shown after being lifted onto a ready-made bed of ties and timbers. It is evident in the picture that the spectators were more numerous than the workmen. Then again, how often are lucky spectators exposed to such magnificent "goings on"? Notice the huge wrecking cable extending from the fire-door and the big opening below the cab deck provided for the application of coal burning equipment (stoker, elevator, etc.) if so desired.

James E. Boynton collection.

Santa Fe's big 250-ton crane is shown drawing the wrecked locomotive out of the creek bottom with its powerful "big hook." The mud clogged engine was pulled back up make-shift spur to siding track shown occupied by a Southern Pacific work train powered by a silver nosed 3700 series engine. This was a spectacular job of locomotive recovery and gives testimony to the ability and imagination of a well-experienced wrecker boss. Cylindrical tank on pilot platform is Elesco feedwater heater, usually mounted on top of the smokebox just ahead of the smokestack. Photographed October 31, 1932.

James E. Boynton collection.

Terrible damage to fireman's side of locomotive is seen in this picture taken October 31, 1932. The engine has been raised onto the special platform and a Santa Fe official looks over the damaged trailer truck. Flood waters have divested the locomotive of her cab and few of the engineman's controls can be recognized. Most of the boiler jacket has been removed and missing asbestos lagging exposes the flexible crown staybolt sleeves and caps on top of the boiler and combustion chamber. Mechanics have just dropped the left main-rod and prepare engine for towing.

James E. Boynton collection.

The big helper engine has turned nearly 90 degrees from its original attitude as shown in this picture taken from the north bank of Tehachapi Creek looking in direction of train movement. Wreckage of the Bear Mountain service station and restaurant can be seen at right side of photograph near the narrow mountain highway. A crew unloads cargo from the overturned Great Northern boxcar and trackmen secure the rails under remainder of train so that it can be moved. Picture taken at Woodford, October 1, 1932.

Robert E. Searle collection.

Normally dry Tehachapi Creek still flows with run-off, the aftermath of a vicious torrent that dumped nearly five inches of rain on the isolated mountain area. View looks downstream and train direction was from right to left in this photograph taken along the creek bottom. A photographer has gained an advantageous position atop the washed out culvert. Brakeman Moore was drowned when he attempted to climb over engine tender to reach the safety of the north bank, but was washed into the roaring flood waters. Woodford, California, October 1, 1932.

Guy L. Dunscomb collection.

This view was taken from the south embankment and looks toward Bakersfield, California. Notice rear of Second 818's train in the upper right background. Tree roots stuck near the front end throttle housing indicate height of flood water after locomotive slid into depression. The fireman's narrow escape from drowning can be easily seen, considering his last tenable position near the engine's smokestack.

Guy L. Dunscomb collection.

This photograph taken several hours after the deluge shows the typical aftermath of flash floods wherein the agent that caused the damage and suffering has disappeared and suggests a nightmare without apparent cause. Seen from downstream, the scouring action of the rough currents on the bedrock is obvious. The husky three-cylinder helper engine can be seen in the retentive grasp of the concrete culvert at the south side of Tehachapi Creek.

Guy L. Dunscomb collection.

Terrible flood damage is shown in this photograph taken from the downstream side of the culvert looking toward Woodford station. Rails and other debris washed from the railroad are shown among the huge boulders strewn along the creek bottom. Engine 5036 and tender are shown in center of picture. Notice two of the four manhole covers on top of the tender are open as though the situation required that it be filled with water.

Gerald M. Best photograph.

In this view looking from the south bank of Tehachapi Creek (westerly train direction) it is quite evident that the helper engine is in need of much help. The erosive effect of the rushing flood waters can be seen in this dramatic photograph taken at Woodford on October 2, 1932.

James E. Boynton collection.

View of derailed tender graphically depicts the extensive damage to the big swing-helper engine after the railroad was washed out from beneath the tracks that supported her. The three-cylinder engine's predicament among the rugged boulders dramatically shows the tremendous job of recovery ahead.

Front end of locomotive displays collection of varied tree roots, branches and other debris that is attached to the pilot and running gear. Law officers were part of the rescue force and their uniforms show that they were of the "old school," suggesting use of motorcycles instead of the more sophisticated cruisers. Rails appearing at upper left side of picture are those of long siding on which Second 818 stood during the flood disaster.

Crushed cab is evident in this picture looking downstream through the rubble deposited on the south side of the culvert. Engineer Alexander Ross, who left the 4-10-2 and ran to a nearby restaurant, was drowned when the little cafe was washed into the flood swollen creek. Fireman Enos A. Brown miraculously escaped the savage waters and lived to survive the horrible nightmare. Shopmen are shown hard at work preparing to rerail the engine's C-2 trailer truck. Notice layers of tree roots clinging to rear of cab and the huge jack supporting the front corner of the firebox. Photo taken in early October 1932.

Gerald M. Best photograph.

The big **Southern Pacific Class** engine has been leveled by means of jacks, wooden blocks, shovels and back breaking labor and preparations are being made to remove the rip-rap that blocks access to her pilot. View is from stream bed looking up toward south abutment. BAK/SJN initials stencilled on the left pilot beam indicates that the locomotive was assigned to the San Joaquin Division with Bakersfield, California her home terminal.

Gerald M. Best photograph.

An ancient Caterpillar employs block and tackle fastened to "deadman" tree at left to drag 220 ton locomotive from south abutment of culvert. It cost nearly $10,000 to repair the big 4-10-2 which was overhauled at the Los Angeles shops.

James E. Boynton collection.

Engine is shown east of culvert after being re-railed and pulled along temporary spur that was built onto creek bed to recover the three-cylinder engine. Mainline side of culvert is again being filled and 5036's tender can be seen above the gondola car in the foreground. Notice downstream dislocation of track on south side of creek and the vintage automobiles parked alongside the old highway over the summit.

James E. Boynton collection.

Welded together in an embrace of no small violence, big three-cylinder 4-10-2 has raised up onto pilot of the pretty Lima built passenger engine 4443. The colorful 4-8-4 was pulling the "Californian" when she collided with heavy freight train being handled by 5015 shown at left. Notice that engine truck of the **Southern Pacific Class** engine has been driven back under the number one drivers and that all of 4443's drivers are derailed. Passenger engine's pilot shroud is wedged under freight engine's cylinders.

W. Beverly Molony collection.

Chapter Four

Head-On at Redlands

The big Golden State Class engine rattled over the east siding switch at Redlands, California, as Engineer Fred G. Toates called "high yellow" across the spacious cab to his fireman. As Fireman Jack Fassett answered the engineer of the westbound *Californian*, he opened the globe valve sending compressed air to ring the bell mounted on the front end of 4443. The big, semi-streamlined 4-8-4, gleaming in her rich, brilliant red, orange and silver trimmings, was pulling train No. 43, a Chicago to Los Angeles passenger train.

It was February 11, 1945 and the *Californian* was making her final approach to the Redlands depot. No. 43 and 44 were a Chicago, Rock Island and Pacific Railroad connection at Tucumcari, New Mexico. The gleaming GS engine was appropriately numbered to match her train numbers.

Redlands boasted two stations. One was on the Redlands branch which left the Southern Pacific mainline at Bryn Mawr, and terminated at Crafton which was ten miles from the junction. Redlands mainline station was a flag stop for No. 43, and this day she had passengers to detrain from the east. The station was almost one-half mile from the east siding switch on tangent main track, and all train movements in this area were controlled by Centralized Traffic Control signal system.

Fassett busily cut down his firing rate to match the engineer's reduction of throttle, and Toates tooled the pretty 4-8-4 locomotive into the little depot to the tune of clattering rods and the dull, methodical clank of the iron bell. The veteran engineer made a perfectly smooth station stop, then became preoccupied making a few minor adjustments to controls in the vestibuled cab. Twisting around and looking back along the riveted side of the huge glossy rectangular tender, the grizzled engineer finally saw the time revered "highball" and uncorked the 300 pounds of steam pressure Fassett had waiting for him. The big Lima built

passenger engine easily accelerated her train, and her barking exhaust flooded the sweetly perfumed orange grove that flanked the siding south of the adjacent mainline track. Train No. 43 swung off the tangent track, nosed into a slight left curve which extended about 15 car lengths, and then reversed toward the right for nearly one-fifth mile to the west Redlands siding switch. The one-fifth mile approach to the west switch was obscured by a small hill about 40 feet high, and Toates was unable to see the west switch until he was approximately five car lengths from it.

For some unknown reason, perhaps because of the distraction of the flag stop this day, both enginemen completely forgot that they had passed a yellow signal at east Redlands siding, an indication that required them to proceed prepared to stop at the next signal. Roaring around the short curve on the approach to the west switch, Toates came off his seatbox with a frightened cry. Instantly he "plugged" his train. If only he had remembered they were "working on yellow," he would have been prepared accordingly. As he rounded the curve, Toates' hair certainly must have raised, for he came out onto straight track at 40 miles-per-hour and found himself staring into the muzzle of a big 4-10-2.

Engine 5015, with Engineer Emmett Bonner at the latch, was about four car lengths west of the west switch, and he had decelerated his train to slow speed for the turnout into the passing track. Bonner was observing a red-over-green signal, permitting him to enter the west end of the siding with his long, heavy freight train. The terrific head-on collision came all too quickly and the big enameled 4400 series locomotive dove under 5015's massive front end with a thunderous roar. The terrible impact drove the heavy *Southern Pacific Class* engine back several car lengths and some freight cars squirted out of her train into the adjoining fruit orchard. The solid pilot shroud on the front end of 4443 gathered up the three-cylinder engine's four-wheel lead truck and rammed it back under the No. 1 drivers. All eight Boxpok driving wheels of the passenger engine hit the ties, as did the 4-10-2's trailer and lead tender truck. Engine 5015's first two sets of drivers were lifted and hung suspended in mid-air, while crude oil seeped into the barrow ditch from the ruptured tender. The *Southern Pacific Class* engine's front end raised into the air in an effort to dissipate some of the awesome force of the violent collision. The two powerful locomotives embraced each other, pressing their smokebox fronts together in a torrid kiss of no small violence. The rear of the freight train was on curved track with helper engines cut in just ahead of the caboose. Seven or eight cars of fuel oil left the train ahead of the helpers, and shot out onto some nearby farmland. This unconventional method of operating trains caused an irate farmer to question the merits of the "Friendly Railroad's" operating procedures.

The train dispatcher was bringing Extra 5015 East to Redlands siding for No. 43 by signal indication, putting the freight train through the "hole" for the *Californian*. This particular incident actually proved that a good fireman, teamed with the fine, steaming qualities of a three-cylinder engine, could be a detrimental factor. Engine 5015's fireboy, Willard Joslyn was firing the big 4-10-2 with a clear exhaust, and this unfortunately helped contribute to the surprise element of the accident. If the big *Southern Pacific Class* locomotive had been making a heavy dark exhaust, it is quite possible that Enginer Toates and his fireman could have seen the black column of smoke rising above the little hummock at the west end of Redlands siding, and reacted in time to stop their fast moving passenger train. The smoke technique was often used under emergency conditions (a violation of railroad operating rules), in train order territory, when an inferior train was trying to get to a siding after it ran out of running time against a superior train. The superior train would spot the inferior train "smoking in," and hold back until it arrived at the passing track. This rather non-professional method of meeting trains was never condoned by carrier officers, and violations were usually met with discipline. Many head-on collisions were actually averted by coloring the exhaust of steam engines, especially when a careless "hogger" found himself on short time, and the opposing superior train right on the "advertised." This practice rapidly became outmoded with the introduction of the comparatively smokeless diesels and the protective signal systems.

The heavy impact of the unscheduled meeting seriously damaged the front end of both loco-motives, but a deadheading baggage-car took the full brunt of the tremendous head-on blow. It was the third car behind 4443, and was nearly doubled over in the middle by compression energy present at the moment of impact. Death in this car was prevented only by virtue of the fact that it was being deadheaded and was therefore unoccupied.

Two factors proved to moderate the freight train's role in the terrific collision. First, Engineer Bonner was moving slowly with 5015, and secondly, since he had his train slack stretched out for a power slowdown at the turnout, the freight train actually absorbed much of the damaging momentum of the *Californian*. This no doubt was a contributory factor in preventing death and serious injury to passengers. Engineer Toates was slammed against the hot gauge-cluttered back head of the 4443's rapidly decelerating boiler. He fought for consciousness as the interior of the spacious cab whirled around in a star-studded blaze of fading light. His hand instinctively reacted to the pain that now contorted his kindly face, and a warm, thick fluid flowed from between his stiffened fingers. Although not seriously hurt, Fred Toates was badly shaken, and he spent several painful days recuperating from his terrible shock. The passenger fireman was suffering from bad bruises as were Bonner and his fireman Joslyn. Bonner's fireman also suffered a broken foot when the three-cylinder engine's cab was crushed by the canted boiler which was deflected upward by the tremendous impact. Luckily, none of the *Californian's* passengers was seriously injured, however a couple who were riding the train were detained for a few days for observation in a local hospital and then released.

Another amazing aspect of this badly arranged meeting of two trains was that Fred Toates was making his last run before retirement. His last trip operating a locomotive was impressive to say the least, even to the extent of producing some mighty spectacular newspaper headlines. Sadly, his last schedule commitment ended a career in a dazzling limelight of notoriety. A final mistake almost ended a half century of engine service in a premature trip to eternity.

Engineer Toates was not to revel in the excitement of the happy faces of his many friends as he brought his train into the station for the last time. Nor was he to thrill to the multitude of flashing photo bulbs that usually illuminated such wonderful occasions. Destiny conned him into making a near fatal error and forced him to slam the swivel mounted throttle lever into the boiler head far short of the planned retirement festivities.

Fred enjoyed his retirement for six or seven years, finally moving to the fabled Indian Valley. This hazy mountain captive valley is the railroaders' heaven and it is here that the misty Rock Candy Mountains of song and myth stand guard over the last terminal in the sky. Head-on collisions are non-existent on this external "pike" and the halcyon beauty of the valley is without limit. Veiled in the shimmering vapors cast aside by his iron steed, the old engineer always reaches the final stop without incident as if guided by the subtle influence of some guiding light. Without fail, Fred always makes a perfect stop at the diminutive cloud shrouded depot close by the cold, crystal clear stream bulging with rainbow trout. The trainmaster in the sky sees to that!

Damage to train No. 43's deadheading baggage car is dramatically shown in this photograph of the Redlands head-on. The terrific compression forces caused by the heavy impact actually bent the all steel car into "U" shape and caused it to partially telescope into the following car. The "Californian" was a Chicago to Los Angeles train that was routed via Rock Island Railroad at Tucumcari, New Mexico. The young lady viewing the wreckage has no doubt concluded that this type of train operation did not include the public's best interests.

W. Beverly Molony photograph.

Tangle of wrecked cars is shown immediately behind engine 5015. A Western Fruit Express refrigerator car was completely destroyed — the sides splitting off around each side of the car ahead and the roof is shown canted against SP "reefer."

W. Beverly Molony photograph.

View of collision looking westward from the west siding switch at Redlands, California. Notice cab of big 4-10-2 which has been crushed against the boiler by its upward deflection. Crude oil from damaged tender seeps into barrow ditch and the first car behind the freight locomotive blocks a public crossing. Fireman W. Joslyn suffered a broken foot and his engineer on 5015, Emmet Bonner, was badly cut and bruised.

W. Beverly Molony photograph.

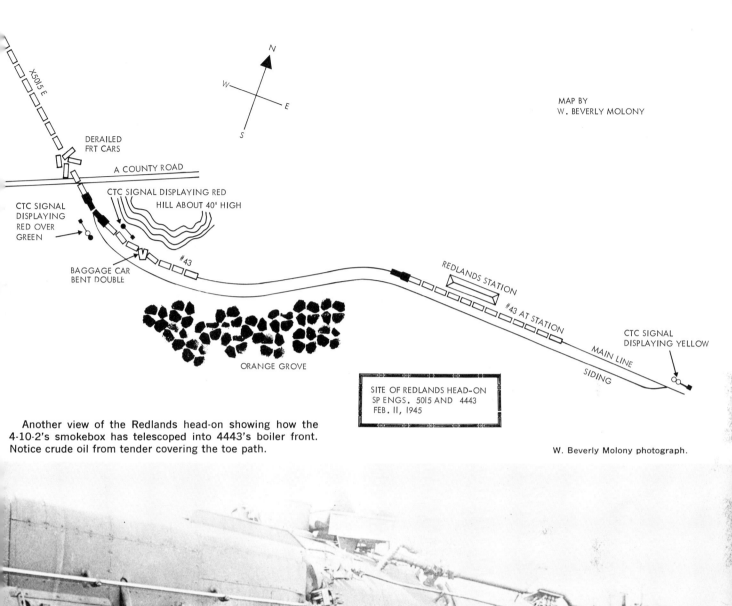

N
W · E
S

MAP BY
W. BEVERLY MOLONY

X5015 E

DERAILED
FRT CARS

A COUNTY ROAD

CTC SIGNAL DISPLAYING RED
HILL ABOUT 40' HIGH

CTC SIGNAL
DISPLAYING
RED OVER
GREEN

BAGGAGE CAR
BENT DOUBLE

#43

ORANGE GROVE

REDLANDS STATION

#43 AT STATION

MAIN LINE

SIDING

CTC SIGNAL
DISPLAYING YELLOW

SITE OF REDLANDS HEAD-ON
SP ENGS. 5015 AND 4443
FEB. 11, 1945

Another view of the Redlands head-on showing how the
4-10-2's smokebox has telescoped into 4443's boiler front.
Notice crude oil from tender covering the toe path.

W. Beverly Molony photograph.

ANOTHER CORNFIELD MEET

A light engine westbound, returning from a helper trip over Beaumont Summit, got punched in the snout by the Golden State Limited at Ordway, California about 10:00 p.m. on August 3, 1934. Engine 4314, a 4-8-2 Mountain type, manned by Engineer A. R. Thomas and Fireman Neal Greene, was helping the passenger train which was moving about 20 M.P.H. when it hit the stationary three-cylinder locomotive. Engine 5024 is shown standing on the main track adjacent to the westbound siding with a spur track shown at far right. The photograph looks eastward at the east end of Ordway siding. The head-on collision took place in San Timoteo Canyon about ten miles east of Colton, California. Ordway had staggered sidings — the westward shown south and to the right of the big helper engine. An eastward siding located on the north side of the mainline (not shown) added to the confusion and a series of curves also contributed to the accident. The Golden State Limited was moving on the main track after meeting a westbound freight train which put her through the eastbound passing track. Both engine crews on the passenger train expected 5024 to be on the siding but soon found themselves involved in a head-on collision. For some unknown reason, 5024's engine crew thought No. 4 was coming down the westbound siding and stayed near the east switch so that they could line back the rails, thus eliminating this additional stop by the Limited.

W. Beverly Molony photograph.

At left is 5024 the light helper engine and on the right is shown 4314 which was doubleheading with another 4-8-2 operated by Engineer C. C. Rice and his fireboy E. L. Parker. Helper engine 4314 was temporarily converted to an 0-8-2 by virtue of the accident — her four wheel engine truck was driven back under her drivers. The valve stem extensions of the 4-10-2 were bent upward by the impact and 4314's cast steel pilot beam and pilot are shown in the foreground. Notice that 5024's pilot beam has assumed the same position as 5015's beam in the Redlands head-on collision. S. G. Scott was engineer on the freight helper engine and Jack Sears was making smoke for him.

W. Beverly Molony photograph.

Head-on view depicts heavy blow that the big Mountain Class passenger engine absorbed when she punched 5024 in the nose! Engine truck bolster is shown in the foreground and is totally demolished. Two truck wheels and axle are derailed amid debris which includes shattered brake cylinder and truck springs. Luckily there were no serious injuries — the helper crew on the three-cylinder engine received the maximum amount of discipline allowable without being discharged. Photograph taken on August 4, 1934 at sunrise.

W. Beverly Molony photograph.

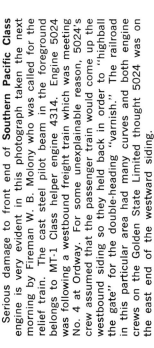

Serious damage to front end of **Southern Pacific Class** engine is very evident in this photograph taken the next morning by Fireman W. B. Molony who was called for the relief train. The cast steel pilot beam in the foreground belongs to MT-1 Class helper engine 4314. Engine 5024 was following a westbound freight train which was meeting No. 4 at Ordway. For some unexplainable reason, 5024's crew assumed that the passenger train would come up the westbound siding so they held back in order to "highball the gate" for the double-heading "varnish." The railroad in this particular area had many curves and both engine crews on the Golden State Limited thought 5024 was on the east end of the westward siding.

This is how the ill-fated locomotive that exploded at Bosque, Arizona appeared shortly after being placed in service on the Sacramento Division. Photograph was made at the Roseville, California roundhouse early in 1927. Notice location of bell and visor-less headlight. The huge cross-head guides were over 8 feet in length. Engine extended 59 feet 4½ inches from pulling face to chafing iron.

Courtesy Southern Pacific Company.

Chapter Five

Disaster at Bosque

Brilliant green flags fluttered in the sooty brackets mounted near the softly lit classification lights indicating that Southern Pacific 5037 was packing the "Irish" for a following section. It was November 11, 1946, and her brightly illuminated train indicators held a sharply silhouetted 4-854, showing that she was the fourth section as she snaked her eastbound manifest out through the inside tracks of the dusty yard at Gila Bend, Arizona. Assigned to the Tucson Division, the three holer had diesel-electric engine 1333 as her helper engine on the point. 1333, a cab-end-type, 1,000 horsepower switcher, was built by the Schenectady Works of the American Locomotive Company in 1942, and she was coupled with her cab end snuggled up against the pilot of the big 4-10-2. This unique combination of motive power was used to muscle the eastbound freight on the fast run between Gila Bend and Tucson, Arizona. The sinister number carried by the diesel certainly could have afforded stimulation for those superstitiously oriented.

The ever quickening exhaust of the huge steamer soon increased to a symphony of stack music as the train assumed the high main iron, hurrying to an unswervable rendezvous with a destiny worse than the environs of hell itself. The odd placement of the locomotives was to cost two engine crews their lives — death's cruel appointment catching them out on the lonely wastes of the Arizona desert.

Engineer Harry S. Hall and Fireman Walter B. Glisson manned the big three-cylinder SP-2 as the 3,175-ton train consisting of 53 loads and three empties left the Gila Bend terminal at 4:00 P.M. The train was soon brought up to about 20 miles per hour by the two locomotives as they headed out toward the low pass in the hazy Maricopa Mountain Range. Fourth 854 had just traversed the southern end of the beautiful Painted Rock Mountains, and had taken on 28,152 gallons of

water at Sentinel, Arizona, about 30 miles west of Gila Bend. The 5037 had an auxiliary water car trained immediately behind her 16,152 gallon tender, a practice not unusual for such operations through this dry, arid country. As they blasted up the 1 per cent grade, the strange off-beat staccato at the three-cylinder engine's stack must certainly have overpowered the crew on the little diesel engine because of their proximity to 5037's front end.

Another *Southern Pacific Class* engine heading Extra 5008 West, handled by Engineer J. E. Vaile and fireman J. A. Ratliff, was in the clear on the siding at Bosque, Arizona. As Fourth 854 approached Bosque, a graceful cloud of dense black oil smoke arched back from 5037's stack, showing that Glisson was sanding out the oil burner's flues. As the double-header roared by, the 5008's three brakemen, R. D. Bonnedum, C. J. Brumbaugh and T. L. Murphy gave her a rolling inspection. Subsequent investigations noted that the head-end crews of the eastbound "hot-shot" were in their regular positions, apparently performing their duties in a normal manner. They certainly did not exhibit any anxieties, nor did they indicate that they were operating subject to any undue pressures. Engine 5037 was not making any excessive amount of smoke continuously which would show that she was being force-fired to alleviate a low water situation in her boiler. Her syncopated exhausts indicated, to trained ears, that she was not being worked any harder than usual for an engine handling such tonnage with a helper engine ahead. After the crews exchanged the time honored "high-balls" and other hand signals, Fourth 854 faded to the east, pounding her way into the hostility of the desolate, but beautiful, southwestern desert.

Suddenly, near a dry wash at milepost 866.36, Fourth 854 came explosively to the end of her scheduled run with a horrible roar that was heard for miles across the stillness of the Arizona wasteland. The big 4-10-2's crownsheet burned and separated from the supporting crown stays and exploded with such fury that some parts of the locomotive were blasted 1,000 feet away from the railroad tracks.

Extra 5008 had just pulled out onto the main track, and Conductor C. W. Birk was standing on the rear platform of the caboose. As he watched the "meet" fade eastward, he was astounded to see one of the most bizarre scenes in his long and varied railroad career. At exactly 4:32 P. M. he saw the head end of Fourth 854 erupt into a huge cloud of smoke, steam, and dust, violently blasting debris in every direction. Only 10.66 miles and 32 minutes out of their Gila Bend terminal, two fine engine crews were engulfed in a horrible atmosphere of superheated steam that made survival an impossibility.

As the ripping firebox sheets released the captive pressure on the boiler water, superheated steam in excess of 225 pounds per square inch instantly roared through the flues of the big boiler. It blasted the front end smokebox door, headlight, bell, and heavy spark netting into the rear of 1333's cab. Her crew was immediately engulfed in a hellish atmosphere of choking, blinding steam and carbon laced with soot-blackened sand. This superheated mixture, plus the unbearable explosive force, would soon prove to be lethal. The tremendous release of pent up energy from the ruptured firebox blew all of the shatterproof glass from 1333's cab windows, and punched the steel shell of the back cab wall nine inches inward at the center. The rear cab door of the little diesel was blown from its hinges, and the metal firewall that separated the cab interior from the diesel engine compartment was sprung forward one and one-half inches. The deadly inferno that occupied the diesel's cab critically injured Fireman Frank Bogulas and blasted Engineer John E. Rhodes out onto the ground. Brakeman T. B. Holoway was found near the locomotive, seriously injured. It is hard to believe that anyone could have survived the concussion and heat of such catastrophic proportions, but Holoway miraculously survived the terrible holocaust, though painfully injured. Sadly, the engine crew of 1333 passed away the next morning in a Tucson hospital, so painfully injured that death's merciful hand was a welcome alternative to the sweet life they knew so well.

The explosive force at the cab end of the huge steamer blasted the firebox end of the boiler upward, catapulting the cab rearward 220 feet west of the point of explosion. The demolished cab crashed to earth 12 feet to the left of the mainline, assuming a 45 degree attitude with its apron and rear eaves resting in the desert sand. Engineer Hall was found a few feet away from the shattered cab, but Glisson was nearly 50 feet to the left. They both perished instantly, because at the exact moment the firebox let go both were sitting only a few feet from the focal point of the explosion.

The terrible upward surge created by the escaping steam tore the boiler from the frame cross-ties that connected it to the running gear; however, the end secured to the smokebox shell temporarily held. The unleashed forces crushed the smokebox into an egg shape, and ripped it from its connection with the cylinder saddle. The steam pipe connection at both cylinders parted, and the delivery pipes from the Bradford front end throttle were broken. After holding momentarily, the riveting at the smokebox connection seam failed, and the rocketing boiler took on new direction. The superheater header was broken away from the boiler connection, but the 50 pipe-like units remained attached to the header. The boiler then virtually peeled itself off of these units that normally extended through the superheater flues from the front to rear flue sheets. The boiler then arched up and over the torn cab of the diesel switch engine in an inverted position with its front end pointed down toward the rails. The superheater units lay twisted and distorted on the engine frame looking much like a jumble of spaghetti awaiting some giant's appetite. The boiler crunched to earth 265 feet east of the point of explosion, breaking out a five-foot section of the right hand rail. The horrible impact of the front flue sheet on the right-of-way depressed the roadbed a full 30 inches. With an ungodly roar, the boiler bounded and landed on its back head (cabless end), upside down, and then re-bounded on its front end again in a huge cloud of lagging, dust, and steam. When the smoke and dust finally cleared, the boiler was located nearly 390 feet from the disaster scene in a reversed position, unbelievably facing the train that she was pulling. The boiler was found resting on its top left side about 17 feet from the right hand rail, partially burying two of the large superheater flues that were torn completely out of the boiler. At the fateful moment of explosion the downward thrust on the front end of 5037 caused the drawbar shank to break, allowing 1333 to continue on as a run-away until she found the depression caused by the falling boiler. Here she derailed in the void, and the No. 3 drivers spun incessantly, showering the roadbed with brilliant red sparks, until the locomotive was shut down by a hostler who came out from Gila Bend. About 80 per cent of the crownsheet, with torn parts of other firebox sheets, was blown down through the bottom of the mud or foundation ring, and finally settled near the dry wash about 65 feet from the north rail and nearly

The boiler and firebox of the ill-fated three-cylinder engine rests 390 feet east of the point of explosion facing (west) toward her train. The boiler is seen on its top left side about ten feet from the south rail and the controls and valves a mere jumble of wreckage amid an endless maze of broken pipes. The reverse lever can be seen just above the fire-door opening and its position on the quadrant indicates that the SP-2 was being operated in a normal manner.

A. B. Pinnell photograph

This locomotive exploded just to the left of the small trestle which was located at milepost 866.36, blasting the crownsheet 66 feet from the mainline track. Notice the telegraph pole that has been separated by the force of the blast. Train direction was from right to left (west to east) and camera view looks southward. These sheets contained approximately 880 staybolt holes and were 3/4 inch steel.

A. B. Pinnell photograph

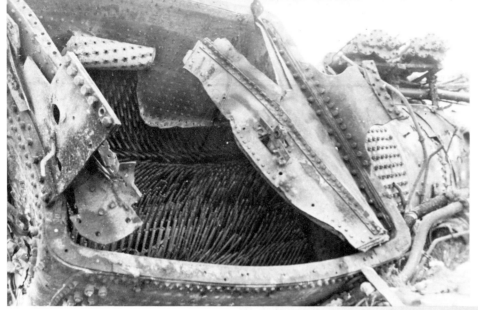

This view of the firebox looks toward the front end of the boiler. Notice the distorted condition (normally rectangular) of the mud-ring that encloses the bottom portion of the firebox. The right side (at center) of the mud-ring was forced outward nearly 7½ inches and the left (lower in photograph) about 7 inches. This distortion has left the mud-ring diamond shape and examination of the photograph shows an 8 inch dent in the back head. Bottom of cross-compound air compressors can be seen at upper right and boiler finally came to rest on its upper left side crushing all three shell courses.

A. B. Pinnell photograph

Front end of boiler showing the front flue sheet and the crater formed when the boiler rebounded off its back head. The large hole at the top of the flue sheet is the broken superheater neck of the boiler connection. Two large superheater flues have been pulled completely from the boiler and one can be seen under the shell. Several flues have been forced through the front flue sheet which was punched in toward the firebox (3 and ¾ inches) when the boiler slammed to earth (265 feet) in its first contact after the lethal explosion.

A. B. Pinnell photograph.

This is the cab-less end of the huge boiler at which Engineer Harry Hall and Fireman Glisson were seated at the time of the deadly explosion. Notice complete destruction to valves, gauges, controls, etc. Glisson's oil firing valve can be seen just above one of the 5½ inch superheater flues buried under the boiler at center of photograph.

A. B. Pinnell photograph.

opposite the point at which the boiler had exploded.

The Worthington feedwater heater and pump combination were located 360 feet ahead of the explosion scene and about ten feet to the left of the main line track. The crownsheet shattered a telegraph pole adjacent to the railroad, and lay mute and ugly on the desert sand, a sad and vivid testimony to the brutal forces unleashed by the tremendous blast. Almost incomprehensible is the fact that this weird episode occupied a time interval of merely a few seconds.

In subsequent investigations initiated by the Interstate Commerce Commission, it was developed that the 5037 was serviced prior to her departure from Gila Bend and that the boiler water concentration of mineral was up to 375 grains per gallon. Engineer E. J. Carter and Fireman J. E. Amos were the inbound crew running the big *Southern Pacific Class* engine and they recalled that they had not experienced any trouble with the boiler feedwater devices or with the boiler water level indicating apparatus. Outside of the pounding in the rods and driver box journals, which was natural for this type of power, nothing out of the ordinary was noticed during their tour of duty on 5037 from Yuma to Gila Bend, Arizona.

During the interval between her arrival at Yuma at 2:05 P. M., and her acceptance by the outbound crew, 5037 was in charge of H. C. Collier who was working as roundhouse foreman at the time. He, along with Machinist H. C. Crown, prepared the hulking 4-10-2 for service and could find nothing wrong with any of the boiler feedwater devices. Visual boiler water level indicating equipment was in proper condition for service, and consequently no maintenance work was done on any of these devices. Perhaps the only thing of unusual nature was the fact that the solids contained in the boiler water were about 125 grains above the concentration allowed by Southern Pacific Company instructions. The Gila Bend area was a bad water district, and 5037's boiler was evidently not blown down to reduce its mineral content to meet the prescribed requirements.

Southern Pacific Company records provided the fact that 5037 had a firebox renewal at the El Paso, Texas General Shops in May of 1941. While undergoing Class 3 repairs in August 1945, the back flue sheet was renewed and a patch (42 inches x 52 inches) was made at the back center of the crown sheet. Another patch (11 inches x 60 inches) was thermal welded into the same crown sheet close to the rear flue sheet.

Other results learned from a precise investigation by the Interstate Commerce Commission inspectors revealed the following cold, cruel facts. The normal configuration of the crown sheet was such that the front portion was seven and ¾ inches higher than it was at the door sheet or rear end. The bottom of the water glasses in the cab of 5037 were installed three and ¾ inches above the highest portion of the crown sheet which allowed for a nominal margin of safety from low water exposing the critical plates. Investigation of the scattered wreckage proved that overheating of the crown sheet had progressed to approximately three inches below the highest portion of the same sheet. For some undetermined reason, the boiler water level was allowed to fall six and ¾ inches below the danger level, causing the extreme temperatures present in the firebox to soften the sheets and allow them to fail. The burned area of the crownsheet was roughly fan shaped as viewed from the top. The widest portion of burn was at the front end converging at a point in the radial staybolts adjacent to the 19th transverse row near the center of the crownsheet. The crownsheet was equipped with 45 transverse rows of supporting stays, and it was found to be burned nearly one-half of the distance to the back head of the boiler. Examination revealed that the fusible (soft plugs) devices had actually functioned, but they failed to prevent the terrible explosion. Was it possible that the plume of smoke from 5037's smokestack as she approached the Bosque siding a result of these soft plugs trying to put out the fire in her boiler? If so, why were Hall and Glisson so complacent during their passage of Extra 5008 West? Past practice and experience had proven that these safety devices, when exposed to prolonged periods of heat, became tempered and nearly reached the same tensile strength as the surrounding plates. This was especially true when they were insulated with scale formed from excessive boiler water solids. In view of these facts, the time interval between fusible plug failure and the actual boiler explosion would have been short indeed.

The four soft plugs in 5037's crownsheet had been renewed about 12 days prior to the explosion, and were in good condition at that time. Records indicated that the three-cylinder giant had experienced a boiler wash at El Paso, Texas on November 7, 1946, just four days before her spectacular accident at Bosque.

Later reports revealed that when the crownsheet pulled off the rounded rivet heads of the staybolts, the metal was cupped over 5/16 of an inch as the sheet pulled by. The staybolt holes in the crownsheet were found to be enlarged and distorted by about 7/8 of an inch in excess of specified diameters, and the 3/8 inch metal plate that formed the crownsheet was drawn out to only 1/8 of an inch in thickness. The tremendous heat and pressure had thinned the crownsheet to only 1/3 of its original thickness, and as this sheet weakened the staybolts lost their grip on the plates and allowed them to fall with devastating explosive force.

Evidence showed that parts of the combustion chamber sheets and the door sheets had pulled away from 880 staybolts, and there were approximately 30 separate tears discernible in these heavy metal plates. The remaining sheets torn from the firebox stays remained attached to the boiler, and the I.C.C. inspector found that 1,606 staybolts had failed. This number roughly approximated half of the total staybolts supporting the entire firebox. A complete study of the debris brought out the following facts that were included in a later report made by the Bureau of Locomotive Inspection. The three (3 and ½ inch) Consolidated safety valves were removed from 5037's remains and installed on engine 5016 for actual testing under steam pressure developed by the sister engine. Engine 5016 was then force-fired and this action resulted in two of the pop valves lifting at the same time, but the boiler pressure never exceeded 226 pounds per-square inch. Force-firing with the blower valve wide open would not cause the No. 3 safety valve to open. After adjusting (screwing down) the two lower pressure safety valves, No. 3 opened at 228 pounds, demonstrating the ability of the Consolidated pop valves to safely regulate the boiler pressure.

The Worthington type 4BL-2 feedwater heater and pump combination with an 8,400 gallon per-hour capacity, was also applied to 5016 for testing. The operating handwheel for 5037's pump throttle valve was found at the disaster scene with the valve stem broken off inside the valve case. Careful dismantling proved the handwheel was set for the ¼ turn open position. With a normal operating pressure of 225 pounds, the damaged pump was adjusted to the same position as found and the pump pulsed at 38 strokes per-minute. This raised the boiler water level 5/16 of an inch in 60 seconds. This adjustment caused the pump to throw about 70 gallons of water per-minute — the pump being capable of a maximum of 80 single strokes per minute at 225 pounds boiler pressure. This important test certainly indicated that 5037's feedwater heater pump was meeting the requirements of normal operating conditions. The only other boiler feedwater device on 5037 was an injector mounted on the fireman's side of the locomotive. The operating levers extending from the cab con-

trol were broken off at the valve stem of the water and overflow valves on the injector body. The valves were found to be in the closed position, denoting that the "gun" was not in use at the time of the catastrophe. It was evident that Glisson had felt that the water pump was supplying his needs or the injector would have been pressed into service to supplement a failing boiler feed situation. It can be seen by examining one photograph taken after the explosion that the reverse lever on the back head of the boiler was still intact. It was in a position "hooked up" toward center, eliminating the use of both water pump and injector in a combination required by extreme steam demand. This undeniable evidence points up and substantiates previous fact that 5037 was being worked at normal capacity.

The tender, tender connections, strainers, shut-off valves etc. were found to be in good condition, properly positioned and unobstructed. The water supply and allied piping was in such condition as to afford a supply of boiler feedwater from the tender to the pump in an uninterrupted manner. Close evaluation of the reflex-type water glass that was attached to the water column on the engineer's side of the locomotive, showed that the reflective surface on the inside of the glass was worn dark to a height of three and one-half inches above the bottom. Experienced enginemen will testify that boiler water in a new reflex-type water glass shows as a darker area than the steam space above it.

Could Engineer Hall have been confused by this worn condition of the reflexes? If so, why was Glisson remiss in not maintaining the safe water level in the boiler by proper reference to the separate reflex glass on his side of the engine? It is very easy to speculate and allow supposition to creep into the overall picture. This question was never answered because the left hand water glass was found badly shattered in the debris, and any evaluation of its condition before the explosion would be inconsequential at best.

At every turn of a compounded paradox, it is evident that the final judgment of all related evidence and pertinent data concerning this horrible disaster come to one precise focus. The engine crew manning the big Alco locomotive was definitely unaware of the fact that they were in nothing but *"Big Trouble."*

The upward flight of S.P. 5037's boiler and firebox has impressed the smokebox shell and pilot platform into a grotesque pile of junk. Explosive displacement of running gear has caused the crosshead to bite into lower guide at forward end of stroke.

James E. Boynton collection.

The ill-fated locomotives are shown in the same relative position as when hauling fourth section of No. 854. Diesel-electric helper engine 1333 was assisting the big 4-10-2 in handling the train over the 1 per cent grades between Gila Bend and Tucson, Arizona. Of the five men operating the two engines, the head brakeman was the only survivor of the catastrophe.

A. B. Pinnell photograph.

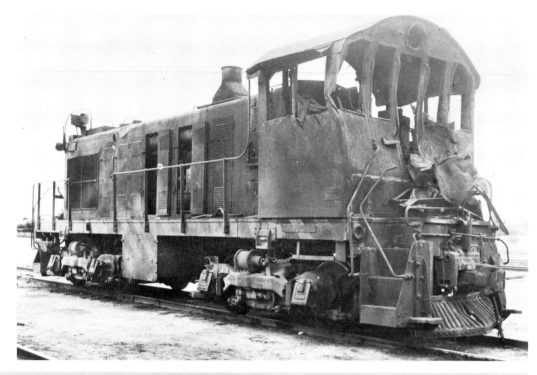

Rear of diesel helper engine wa coupled to smokebox end of ex ploding boiler of 4-10-2. The forc of the tremendous energy releas has blown all the shatterproof glas to cab interior and blasted cab wa inward. Green flag can be seen i the holder above the classificatio lamps.

A. B. Pinnell photograph.

This picture looks east toward the Maricopa Mountains which was i the direction of train movement anc shows roof of big 4-10-2's cab tc left of right-of-way. Square openin in roof was normally occupied by a hinged ventilator cover that allowec heat and smoke to escape from locomotive cab. This cab was blast ed 220 feet west of the point o explosion, killing both enginemen in stantly. Final measurements prover the cab and boiler to be separatec by a distance of 610 feet.

A. B. Pinnell photograph.

When the boiler landed on the back head an 8 inch depression was formed causing complete distortion of the firebox and mud-ring. This view shows underside of boiler and firebox and looks west toward train.

A. B. Pinnell photograph

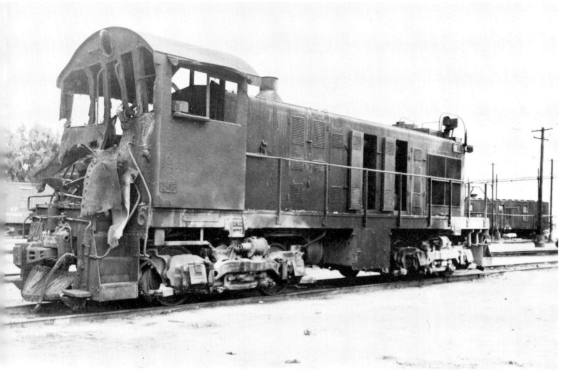

The anti-spark netting and parts of the smokebox door from steam engine is shown appended to rear cab and platform of diesel helper engine. Mineral staining from the exploding boiler has progressed to front of 1333, indicating extent blast projected boiler water from ruptured firebox. Rear cab wall was compressed inward about 9 inches.

A. B. Pinnell photograph.

Locomotive cab once occupied the void appearing just ahead of the tender. The sandbox holding the "real estate" used to scour out the flues has been dented by the blast that came out the fire-door in the cab. The firepan was blasted down onto the trailer truck frame breaking it in two places. Later investigation showed that the tender and all of its connections were in good condition and offered an uninterrupted supply of boiler feedwater.

A. B. Pinnell photograph.

This photograph was taken inside the inverted boiler and looks toward the rear flue sheet from locomotive cab. The 5½ inch flues held the 50 unit superheater pipes and the mass of crownstays once supported the missing crownsheet. Forward portion of the crownsheet with soft plugs has been blown down into combustion chamber just to rear of smaller fire-tubes. So tremendous was the force that blew this portion of crownsheet onto the combustion chamber sheets that the plates made an impression one and ¾ inches deep. Three of the four drop plug thimbles can be seen near top of photograph.

A. B. Pinnell photograph.

Three-cylinder engine's cab is shown where it came to rest in the desert sands near Bosque, Arizona after the terrible boiler explosion of November 11, 1946. Fireman Glisson was found 58 feet from the cab and one of the enginemen's coats has been carefully hung from the bottom of the damaged cab. Hinged cab ventilator cover can be seen in center foreground of picture.

A. B. Pinnell photograph.

This photograph shows left side running gear of engine and looks toward front of blasted locomotive. The 50 superheater units can be seen where they finally came to rest after the boiler literally peeled itself off of them. These units passed through the big superheater flues and extended to the rear flue sheet where they made a tight bend and returned to the superheater header (a distance of 23 feet six inches). Steam from the boiler was routed through these pipes and hot gasses and fire flowing toward the smokestack imparted a high degree of temperature to the steam with a resultant increase in power and efficiency.

A. B. Pinnell photograph.

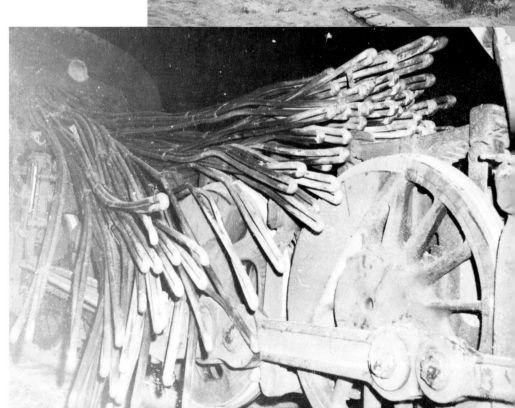

This excellent night photograph shows the crushed smoke-box shell which was canted forward when the boiler left the engine frame and sailed over the diesel helper engine. The rivet holes at the smokebox connection seam have been distorted by the tremendous force of the explosion and the steam pipe connection to the right hand cylinder has been broken. Crosshead for center engine can be seen above upper crosshead guide for right outside gear.

A. B. Pinnell photograph.

Head-on view shows portion of steam engine that was snuggled up against cab of the little diesel helper engine. Steam pipe to left steam chest has been broken at Bradford front end throttle and the pilot platform has been bent by downward thrust of the smokebox shell. Notice broken drawbar shank at center of pilot beam.

A. B. Pinnell photograph.

Badly damaged cab is viewed from bottom in this photo-graph that looks west along mainline. The catapulting action of the exploding boiler has ripped cab braces, steam and air piping and other connections to boiler. A seatbox can be seen at the lower left side of photograph.

A. B. Pinnell photograph.

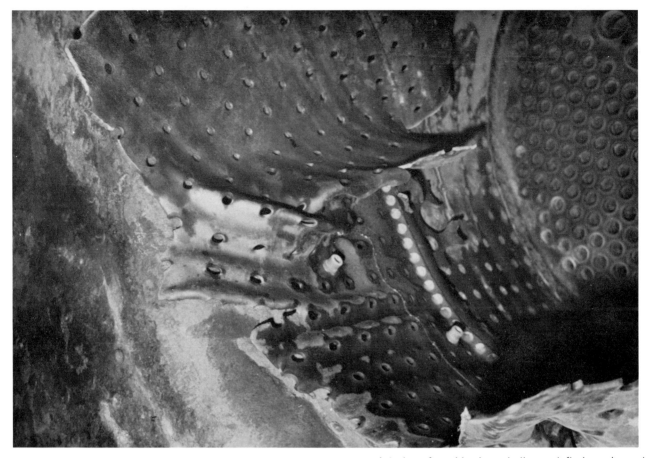

Interior of upside down boiler and firebox shows two of the four "soft plug" thimbles tapped into the front portion of the crownsheet. The crownsheet was blown from its normal position above the large flues at top right down onto the sheets at bottom of combustion chamber. The crownsheet came down with such force that it left an impression 1 and ¾ inches deep. The line of rivets just ahead of the No. 1 drop plug marks the joining of the crown and rear flue sheets.

A. B. Pinnell photograph.

View looks from cab end of locomotive toward front end showing the firepan which has been blown down onto trailer truck frame. Shattered firebrick is seen scattered throughout the remains of the locomotive framework.

Collection of Robert J. Church.

The distorted condition of the smokebox shell is vividly seen in this photograph taken of missing smokebox front. The train indicators still carry 4-854. Steam delivery pipe to left steam chest has parted at front end throttle connection. Notice missing drawbar head which was broken from shank by explosive pressures at time of crownsheet failure.

A. B. Pinnell photograph.

Scorched paint on the rear cab plates gives testimony of the tremendous heat produced by the blast. Netting and other debris from the front end of the three-cylinder locomotive can be seen on the rear platform of the helper engine. Rear cab door and headlight have been torn from engine and front cab glass has been blown to oblivion.

A. B. Pinnell photograph.

Point of explosion was at a dry wash 866.36 miles from Southern Pacific's General offices in San Francisco, California. Notice compression of ballast, cracked concrete footing under trestle and scattered brick from firebox of big 4-10-2.

Train was proceeding from right to left in photograph which looks southward and engine's crownsheet lies about 50 feet behind photographer.

A. B. Pinnell photograph.

Showing no trace of its shattering experience, the 5037 is shown at Tucson, Arizona, with 2-904 showing green signals. The only clue to the new boiler is the lack of large smoke box door hinges. These were later added. July 3, 1949.

W. C. Whittaker Collection

Her last mile has ended at the scrapper's spur. The boiler that is about to be cut from her frame was the second that was applied because of her unfortunate accident at Bosque, Arizona in 1946. Note that the smokebox door hinges have been reinstalled. Water stains from leaking flexible stay-bolts coats firebox surface and trailer truck frame. Photograph taken at Portland, Oregon in April 1954.

Larry Harrison photograph.

Diary of a Three-Cylinder Locomotive Engineer

I went firing on the Los Angeles Division of the Southern Pacific on July 13, 1918 after my graduation from High School at Colton, California. Most of my railroad experience until I went on passenger in 1958 was spent in and around Colton. I worked in helper service and on mainline locals between Colton and Indio, California (72 miles) and I had lots of experience on the 5000 Class engines before and after my promotion to locomotive engineer in June 1936. The 4-10-2's were good steaming engines and they gave the engine crews a very smooth ride when in good repair. The light fires were much easier to adjust when drifting down the grades after making a helper trip. The six exhausts which were produced when using the drifting throttle created a much more even draft than that generated by a two bore engine.

The throttles on this type of power were hard to adjust, particularly the first opening movement. It was a front end throttle but not of the multiple valve type* that became standard on the larger locomotives. There was one large valve with a very unsatisfactory initial pilot valve which was supposed to open enough to build a balancing pressure underneath the main throttle opening. Obviously, without a balancing chamber the valve did not operate as easily as it was supposed to.

The greatest fault in design of the three-cylinder locomotives was the middle engine's inaccessibility. The center main rod was comparatively short in respect to most outside the frame rods, which fact caused them to wear their brasses faster than the outside rod bushings. After a general overhaul they rode like a passenger car. As parts of the running gear became worn, the ride would roughen up and a bad slam-bang would

develop under the engine. Their exhaust tune when lame was very distinctive and could best be described as a hop, skip and jump rhythm. The middle valve received its motion entirely from the outside valve stems and any wear in the outside gear was doubled by the time it actuated the middle valve. In experimenting while running these engines light with badly worn valve gears, you could at slow speeds, of about ten miles-per-hour, "hook the engine up" to a point where the center valve would not be moved to admit any steam to the middle cylinder. The locomotive then became a two-cylinder "job" and the center engine did nothing as far as the production of power was concerned. As speed picked up, there would be enough inertia imparted by the outside gear so that the moving parts would take up the slack and force the middle valve to move far enough to uncover the steam ports.

I made my first trip running in June 1936 on the 5013 while handling a fruit block east from Indio, California to Yuma, Arizona. The return trip was on the same engine but via the Inter-California Railroad which dipped down into Mexico just about six miles west of Yuma at Araz Junction, Arizona. It was a 62 mile run through Mexico to the Mexicali-Calexico border crossing and then up through the Imperial Valley to connect with the mainline at Niland, California and then on to Indio. Shortly after our mainline between Indio and Yuma was C.T.C.* equipped (1956) the Inter-California Railroad tracks were removed from Pasqualitos, Mexico (about 10 miles east of Mexicali) to Araz Junction. The original mileage from Niland to Araz Junction was nearly 97 miles and the railroad had been built between May 1902 and July 1911.

My first bad breakdown with these engines occurred in January 1937 on engine 5038. I was

---

American Throttle Company produced the multiple throttle valve designed with a balancing chamber allowing for easier and finer adjustment.

Centralized Traffic Control.

on the hard pull approaching Araz Junction from the old Inter-California Railroad with 136 cars of lettuce. A bad pound developed under the engine and I thought all of the gauges were going to jump off the boiler head. Luckily I had previously been firing on an engine that had acquired the same symptoms and it proved to be a broken crank pin on the middle engine. It had broken a short distance inside one of the crank arms but did not tear loose. I eased off on the throttle to lessen the pound and got down on each of the gangway ladders to see what was wrong. From there I could observe that both the right and left number 2 drivers had the same degree of wobble indicating, I thought, that the same conditions existed as in the previous experience. Right at the point where the pound began, the grade tipped over the apex of a summit and by nursing 5038 along for about 50-car lengths, I was able to get the train to a point from which it would roll (about five miles) to a stop short of the bridge over the Colorado River at Yuma. From there the yard crews got the train into the yard and subsequent inspection showed that it actually was a broken crank pin as had occurred before.

I never had an experience with side rod failures on these 4-10-2's but I very well understood that both number 1 side rods were never to be disconnected at the same time. This would allow the offset axle on the number 1 drivers to get out of time with the center main rod. This very bad situation would allow the center main rod to destroy itself and the number 1 driver axle, contributing to the ruination of the middle engine and possible derailment of the locomotive and train.

I went into passenger service in 1958 pulling trains 1 and 2, the Sunset Limited. This beautiful train ran between Los Angeles, California and New Orleans, Louisiana and I handled her from Los Angeles to Yuma, a distance of 251 miles. In 1964 when trains 1 and 2 were consolidated with 3 and 4, the Golden State Limited, a Los Angeles to Chicago train, the schedules created a 25 hour layover at Yuma. I then displaced on 39 and 49, the Kansas City train, and remained on that job until it was discontinued in August of 1967. I then "bumped" on a 9:00 A.M. local freight that worked the Kaiser Steel Company train yard at Fontana, California. We handled the interchange work between the Southern Pacific and the Kaiser Railroad crews at the steel plant. My last trip was on August 14, 1967 even though I had wanted to work until September 6, 1968 at which time I would have completed 50 years of service. I had been number 1 engineer on the Los Angeles Division seniority roster for three years and I enjoy my retirement very much. I do miss the feel and throb of a real live steamer under my feet.

Speaking of steam. I made my last steam trip on engine 4179 on August 9, 1955. She was a cab-ahead 4-8-8-2 of the AC-8 Class and she had been built by the Baldwin Locomotive Works in 1939. I had 4179 on a helper trip from Colton to Beaumont and then returned to Colton. My last trip on a three-cylinder engine of the 5000 Class was also a Colton to Beaumont helper with locomotive 5021. That was on January 31, 1953 and this engine was later presented to the Southern California Chapter of the Railway and Locomotive Historical Society for all time preservation. Southern Pacific 5021 is now (1971) stored in running condition at the Santa Fe roundhouse in San Bernardino, California and it is hoped that this engine will be used for movies or an occasional steam fan trip.

W. Beverly Molony
Southern Pacific Railroad Engineer
Retired.

Big SP-2 sits in the "hole" while meeting the Sunset Limited which is powered by 4309, a 4-8-2 Mountain type passenger locomotive. The 4-10-2 heads a westbound manifest at Palm Springs, California in 1942.

Walter H. Thrall photograph. Don Duke collection.

Appendix

Glossary

ARTICULATED. A locomotive having two sets of cylinders, driving independent groups of wheels, which support two sets of frames, joined by a hinge or pivot point. The leading set of frames, cylinders and driving wheels support the forward end of the boiler and swivel radially about the pivot connection, giving the effect of a truck, thus reducing the rigid wheelbase. In compound, articulated locomotives (true Mallet) the usual arrangement is to drive the rear section by high-pressure cylinders and the front by the low-pressure cylinders. In single-expansion, articulated locomotives all cylinders receive steam at boiler pressure.

ARTICULATED CONSOLIDATION (SOUTHERN PACIFIC RAILROAD). A group of steam locomotives of the 2-8-8-2, 2-8-8-4 and 4-8-8-2 wheel arrangement, used on the Pacific Lines. AC-1 to AC-3 (4000 to 4048) — AC-4 to AC-8 (4100 to 4204) — AC-9 (3800 to 3811) — AC-10 to AC-12 (4205 to 4294).

AUXILIARIES (LOCOMOTIVE). Appurtenances other than the main locomotive cylinders using boiler steam. Examples: Air compressor, feedwater heater pumps, dynamo, injector, blowers, etc.

BACK-PRESSURE GAUGE. A steam pressure gauge that registers back pressure in the exhaust cavities of a locomotive's cylinders. By proper control of this pressure, the locomotive can be worked economically without referral to other devices.

BACK HEAD (BOILER). The plate forming the back end of a boiler and in which the fire door opening is placed. It is separated from the back firebox sheet by the back water space. Sloping back heads are largely used to increase the grate area and provide more room in the locomotive cab.

BARREL, BORE, HOLE (SLANG). Cylinder of an engine; also boiler shell.

BERKSHIRE. A steam locomotive having 2-8-4 wheel arrangement (see Whytes Classification). First used in 1925 on the Boston & Albany Railroad.

BIG BOY (LOCOMOTIVES). A group of 25 articulated consolidation steam locomotives used on the Union Pacific Railroad having the 4-8-8-4 wheel arrangement. They were the largest two engine simple articulateds ever built (total engine weight 722,250 lbs.) and were numbered 4000-4024 (ALCO 1941-1944).

BIG HOOK. A locomotive crane or derrick used to lift wrecked railroad equipment, etc.

BLACK DIAMONDS (SLANG). Coal used to fire steam locomotives.

BLOWER. A device regulated by a valve in the locomotive cab used to create a draft thereby stimulating the fire. Steam is piped to the exhaust nozzle tip and the resultant discharge causes a vacuum in the smokebox drawing oxygen into the firebox.

BLOW-OFF VALVE. A valve having a large opening which is screwed into the water leg of the firebox, but sometimes into the back head above the crown sheet. The valve is opened to carry off scale, mud, mineral and other solids formed by the boiling of water.

BOILER BEARING. A casting secured to the top of the frames of the leading unit of an articulated locomotive, and upon which the forward end of the boiler is carried by means of a sliding bearing. This device is sometimes referred to as the articulation table.

BOILER BEARING PLATE. A metal plate, usually of steel, forming the bearing surface between the boiler-bearing saddle and the boiler-bearing casting of an articulated locomotive.

BOILER BEARING SADDLE. A casting, the top part of which is shaped to fit the boiler shell to which it is attached, the bottom surface being flat and attached to the boiler bearing plate. It transmits through the boiler bearing the weight of the forward portion of the boiler to the leading unit of an articulated locomotive.

BOILER HEAD. See BACK HEAD.

BOILER JACKET. A covering of thin sheet iron over the lagging of a locomotive boiler, cylinder or other protected radiating surface.

BOOSTER. An auxiliary engine for driving the locomotive trailing truck wheels or tender truck wheels, thus adding tractive force to the locomotive. It may be engaged or disengaged as conditions require. Maximum engaging speed 12 M.P.H; maximum operating speed 21 M.P.H.

BOXPOK. A cast steel driving wheel center utilizing box-section spokes and rim. It was produced by General Steel Casting Corporation and was principally designed to reduce dynamic augment.

BUG (SLANG). The semi-automatic key used by an expert telegrapher and used to transmit or receive Morse code messages. Ordinary telegraph keys are not "bugs."

BUILDER'S NUMBER, SHOP NUMBER. A serial number assigned to a locomotive during erection. This number is usually cast onto a bronze or similar metal plate along with the date of construction and other pertinent data. One plate is usually mounted on each side of a steam locomotive's smokebox or cylinders.

BUMPED. A term referring to a worker who exercises his seniority to displace another worker who is below him on the list. This process continues until the man at the bottom of the roster is bumped, thereby becoming unemployed.

BUSHING. A lining for a hole. It usually consists of a cylindrical ring which forms a bearing surface for some other object. This other object can be a shaft, valve, crank, pin, etc. which is inserted into the ring.

CAL. P. (CALIFORNIA PACIFIC RAILROAD). A railroad incorporated in 1865 and completed from Vallejo, California, to Sacramento and Marysville in 1869. Central Pacific Railroad took over this railroad at an early date and Southern Pacific uses portions of the original railroad between Sacra-

mento and San Francisco which were absorbed into the system in 1898.

CANNON (SLANG). A hand gun or pistol.

C.T.C., CENTRALIZED TRAFFIC CONTROL. A block signal system under which train movements are authorized by block signals whose indications supersede the superiority of trains for both opposing and following movements on the same track.

CHAIN GANG (SLANG). Freight pool crews used first in and first out of terminals. They follow each other in strict, sequential order much as if they were chained together like the prisoners of the old Southern penal systems.

CLASSIFICATION LIGHTS, LAMP. Lamps usually attached to the sides of the locomotive smokebox designating the class of train handled by the locomotive, i.e., White lenses — extra train. Green lenses — displaying signals for a following section of regular train. Lamp extinguished — regular train.

CONSOLIDATION (SOUTHERN PACIFIC RAILROAD). A group of steam locomotives of the 2-8-0 wheel arrangement used over the entire system. Pacific Lines consolidation engines occupied the 2500, 2600, 2700 and 2800 numbering series.

CONSTRUCTION NUMBER. See builders number.

COUNTERBALANCE. The weight or mass of metal applied to one part of a driving wheel center to balance the revolving weights of the crank pin, main or side rod, and the reciprocating weights of the crosshead, piston and piston rod.

CRANK. A device for converting rotary motion to reciprocating motion or vice versa. It consists of a crank arm, one end of which is attached to a shaft, while the other end is free to rotate about the axis of the shaft.

CRANKPIN. A short cylindrical shaft fastened to a crank on a driving wheel, or joining the two webs or discs of a crank axle.

CROSSHEAD GUIDES. A bar or bars that are positioned parallel to the axis of a cylinder and piston rod, forming ways or slides in which the crosshead moves. Also called slides.

CROSSTIE. A transverse brace for strengthening a locomotive or truck frame.

CROWNSHEET. A sheet or plate placed directly over the fire and forming the roof of a firebox. It is exposed to an intense heat on one side and covered with water on the other and there is a violent formation of steam on its surface.

CROWN STAY. A staybolt connecting the crownsheet of a boiler with the roof sheet. It performs the same functions for the crownsheet as the staybolt does for the side sheets.

CYLINDER. A casting forming a chamber whose ends are circular, with straight parallel sides, as the cylinder of a steam engine.

CYLINDER HEAD COVER, CASING. A casing of sheet iron or steel iron or steel used over the cylinder heads to protect the lagging from damage and to give the cylinders a neat appearance.

CYLINDER SADDLE. That part of a cylinder casting on which the smokebox rests and contains the steam and exhaust passages, is called a half saddle. In very large engines the saddle is sometimes cast separately and bolted to the cylinders through flanges on each.

CRYING ROOM (SLANG). A railroad crew register room that acts as a catalyst toward the production of interminable grievances. This also causes the so-called "caboose lawyers" to become eloquent in regard to inequities established soon after the arrival of Christopher Columbus.

DEADHEAD. A railroad employee or railroad equipment being moved to another location without performing any revenue service.

DENVER & RIO GRANDE WESTERN RAILROAD 3 CYLINDER 4-8-2's. A group of ten Mountain Class locomotives built by Baldwin Locomotive Works in 1926. Designated as M-75, the engines had three (25" x 30") cylinders, 67" drivers and a total weight of 419,310 pounds.

DOOR SHEET. The back sheet of the firebox. It is this sheet that contains the fire door.

DROP 'ER DOWN. The action whereby the engineer drops or moves the reverse level down on the quadrant toward full power position. This causes locomotive to use steam through the full stroke and results in maximum use of steam and water. The fireman usually reacts by increasing the amount of fuel burned and supplies an increased volume of feedwater to satisfy the heavier demand for steam.

DRY PIPE. A pipe conveying steam from the throttle valve in the dome to the steam pipes in the smokebox. It is usually placed inside the boiler and supported by hangers riveted to the boiler shell, but on some locomotives it has been placed outside and along the top of the boiler.

DYNAMIC AUGMENT. That force produced by the centrifugal action of the portion of the driving-wheel counterbalance weight added to oppose the thrust of the reciprocating parts, and acting in a direction perpendicular to them. This force, when exerted downward, increases the pressure of the wheel on the rail, and when acting upward tends to lift the wheel from the rail.

DYNAMO. A machine for generating electricity, driven by a small engine or turbine mounted on the boiler or smokebox to supply current to an electric headlight, cab lights, etc.

DYNAMOMETER CAR. A car equipped with apparatus for measuring and recording drawbar pull, horsepower, brake-pipe pressure, and other data, connected with locomotive performance and train haul conditions.

EXHAUST SPLITTER. A device applied over the smokestack of a steam locomotive, used to divert the damaging flow of exhaust steam and smoke in a lateral direction. This apparatus helps eliminate damage to the roof of snowsheds and tunnels.

EXPANSION JOINT (STEAM). A joint in a steam pipe so constructed that the pipe can vary its length and position while remaining steam-tight. It consists of two pipes, one of which fits inside the other. The outside pipe contains a stuffing box in which packing rings are fitted around the inside pipe and held in place by a gland.

EXTENDED SMOKEBOX. A smokebox which extends out beyond the cylinder saddle and which has a large volume. It provides a space for the accumulation of sparks. Within certain limits, extending the length of the smokebox amplifies the draft.

F CLASS (SOUTHERN PACIFIC). A group of steam locomotives of the 2-10-2 wheel arrangement used over the entire system. Pacific Lines engines of this class carried designations from F-1 through F-6 (3600 to 3769).

FEEDWATER HEATER. A device by means of which the heat in the waste gasses from the firebox or exhaust steam can be transferred to the boiler feedwater before it is delivered to the boiler for evaporation.

FIREBOX. The furnace or box in which the fuel is burned.

FIRE BRICK. A special kind of brick made of refractory material to resist a high degree of heat. It is used in oil-burning locomotives to form a surface against which the burning oil may impinge. This surface is commonly referred to as the flash wall.

FIREPAN. A pan made of sheet iron or steel, lined with fire brick and fitted to the bottom of the firebox of an oil-burning locomotive. It serves the same purpose as the ashpan on a coal burning engine.

FLAG STOP. An unscheduled stop where a passenger train could be flagged so that passengers may be entrained or detrained. Designated in timetable as *Flag Stop.*

FLEXIBLE STAYBOLT. A staybolt designed to allow the slight relative movements due to expansion and contraction of the plates which it secures. This arrangement prevents shearing and bending stress in the bolt, thus preventing its failure.

FLUE. The fire tubes of a locomotive boiler are often designated as flues, but since the introduction of the superheater the ordinary small fire tubes are called *Tubes.* The large tubes containing the superheater units are commonly called *Flues.*

FLUE SHEET. Also known as *Tube Sheet.* A plate or sheet forming one end of a locomotive boiler shell and having a large number of holes in which the ends of the tubes are inserted. The plate next to the smokebox is called the front tube sheet and that next to the firebox the back tube sheet.

FOUNDATION RING, MUD RING. A steel casting or an iron or steel bar shaped to correspond to the ground plan of a firebox, rounded at the corners, separating the inside and outside sheets of the firebox, and to which these sheets are riveted.

FOUNTAIN, TURRET. A distributing chamber or steam head secured on top of the boiler, inside or near the cab, having one main valve for opening or closing communication with the steam in the boiler and a number of outlets serving the auxiliaries.

FRUIT BLOCK. A train of refrigerator cars hauling fruits or vegetables to the early eastern markets.

Because of the perishable nature of the commodity, special handling is usually given to this type of freight train.

FUSIBLE PLUG. A plug screwed into a brass thimble in a crown sheet, made of an alloy of lead, tin and bismuth. The proportions give the alloy a melting point somewhat higher than the temperature of the water surrounding the plugs, corresponding to the steam pressure carried. Sometimes known as *Soft Plugs* or *Drop Plugs.* When a soft plug fails or drops, a jet of water and steam is directed onto the fire putting it out, thereby preventing an explosion.

GLOBE VALVE. A valve with a spherical or globular shaped body, usually having a disk with a conical edge seating in a ring similarly ground to fit the disk. The spindle or stem that raises and lowers the disk has a thread on it working in a nut.

GOLDEN STATE CLASS (SOUTHERN PACIFIC). A group of steam locomotives of the 4-8-4 wheel arrangement used over the entire system. Later known as "General Service" class. Pacific Lines engines of this class were officially designated as GS-1 through GS-8 (4400 to 4488).

GONS (SHORT FOR GONDOLA). An open-top railroad car usually used for bulk loading. Named after a boat of similar design used to ply the waters of Venice, Italy.

GRATE AREA. The product obtained by multiplying the length by the width of a locomotive grate. Expressed in square feet.

GUN (SLANG). See injector.

HACK (SLANG). Caboose or cabin car.

HEATER (SLANG). A pistol or similar handgun.

HIGHBALL (SLANG). A proceed signal given by hand or lantern signal. The term is derived from the old-time station signal that consisted of a huge ball secured to a rope. When it was not desired to stop a train, the agent raised the ball to the uppermost limits of the rope, thereby indicating to the approaching engineer that a stop was unnecessary.

HOGGER. A locomotive engineer or engineman. Also known as a pig jockey, hog mauler, eagle eye, runner, or hoghead.

HOLE (SLANG). A siding track, passing track, or any track auxiliary to the mainline and used for meeting or passing trains.

HORSEPOWER. A term used as a measure of power. One horsepower is equivalent to a force necessary to raise 33,000 pounds one foot in one minute.

HOOKING UP. A term meaning to readjust the steam locomotive reverse level thereby regulating the valve cut-off. This allowed the engine to use steam expansively thus increasing the train speed and provided for economical operation of the locomotive. The opposite of "drop 'er down."

INJECTOR. A device for forcing water into a steam boiler in which a jet of steam imparts its velocity to the water and forces it into the boiler against the steam pressure.

INTERCEPTING VALVE. A device used on compound locomotives and located in the saddle of the left high-pressure cylinder between the receiver and the exhaust passages of the high-pressure cylinders. In starting a train, the locomotive uses live steam from the boiler in all cylinders. When the pressure in the receiver rises above the amount to which the reducing valve is adjusted, the valve automatically closes and cuts the live steam off from the receiver. The locomotive is thus changed to compound automatically. The engineman can forestall this compounding by use of an emergency valve located in the cab.

INTERLOCKING. An arrangement of signals and signal appliances so interconnected that their movements must succeed each other in proper sequence, and for which interlocking rules are in effect. It may be operated manually or automatically.

IRON CROSS. Nickname for Atchinson, Topeka & Santa Fe Railroad. The Santa Fe medallion as applied to its equipment closely resembled the old German medal.

IRON HORSE. Railroad locomotive. Term is of Indian origin.

JACKET. See *Boiler Jacket*.

JOURNAL. That part of an axle or shaft on which the journal bearing or brass rests. The part of a crank axle on which the driving-box brass rests is called the main journal to distinguish it from the crank-pin journal.

LATCH (SLANG). Locomotive throttle.

LATERAL DRIVING BOX. A driving box used on large steam locomotives that yielded laterally on curved track thereby reducing the total rigid driving wheelbase.

LIMA. Lima Locomotive Works at Lima, Ohio.

M. A Southern Pacific tonnage unit in 1,000-pound divisions. Derived from the Roman numeral M denoting 1,000.

MAIN ROD. A large iron or steel rod of rectangular or "I" section, pivoted at one end to the crosshead wrist pin and at the other to the main crank pin. It transmits the motion of the piston and piston rod to the driving wheel.

MALLET (MALLIES). See Articulated Compound.

MANIFOLD. A series of steam valves with allied piping arranged on the fireman's side of the cab and used by him to control the various auxiliaries using steam. It is by proper use of the manifold that the fireman adjusts the firing rate of the locomotive.

MIKE (SLANG). Nickname for the Mikado or 2-8-2 type locomotive. Southern Pacific Railroad Mikado engines used in the Pacific Lines were numbered 3200 to 3324 with a few vacant numbers in the series. They covered class MK-2 through MK-11 and were known as McArthur's during World War II.

MOUNTAIN TYPE 4-8-2 (SOUTHERN PACIFIC RAILROAD). A series of steam locomotives officially designated at MT-1 through MT-5 and numbered 4300 through 4376, 4385 through 4390.

NAME PLATE, BUILDER'S PLATE. A cast iron or brass plate commonly fastened on each side of the smoke-box giving the name of the builder, date of construction, and the builder's number of the locomotive.

NATHAN CHIME WHISTLE. A pleasantly tuned steam whistle built by the Nathan Manufacturing Company of New York, New York. The whistle sound was soft and non-irritating at close range, but could be heard for many miles.

OIL REGULATOR, FIRING VALVE. A valve with an extension handle running to the cab, placed in the oil supply pipe and used to regulate the amount of oil supplied to the burner according to the demand for steam.

OXYACETYLENE, ACETYLENE TORCH. A torch that combines oxygen and the highly inflammable hydrocarbon gas acetylene to produce a flame of intense heat. It is used either to burn metal or to combine and fuse metal in a thermal weld.

PER CENT GRADE. The amount of vertical climb a track assumes in 100 linear feet. If a track raises two feet in a hundred foot linear run, the gradient is two per cent.

PILOT SHROUD. A heavy metal covering, shield or shroud used in place of the old conventional locomotive pilots. Used on the modern locomotive as a means of streamlining its appearance.

PISTON VALVE. A spool-shaped casting of iron or steel moving forward and backward in a cylindrical valve chamber formed in a steam chest for admitting steam to and exhausting it from a locomotive cylinder.

PLUGGED (SLANG). Initiation of an emergency application of the train airbrakes. Also known as *Big Hole, Wipe The Clock, Clean The Gauge* or *Plug 'er.*

PYROMETER (STEAM). An electrical temperature indicator that shows the true temperature of steam in the steam chest. It helps the enginemen to obtain the most economical and efficient operation of a superheated locomotive and operates on the thermocouple principle.

QUADRANT. A notched sector along which the reverse lever moves, and which by means of a latch holds the lever at any particular point to regulate the point of cut-off of the valves. A quadrant is also used for a throttle lever.

REAL ESTATE (SLANG). Sand used on the rails to increase the locomotive's adhesion and to prevent spinning or sliding driver wheels. Also introduced to firebox of hard working locomotive thereby cutting the insulating carbon from the tubes and flues and increasing the engine's capacity to steam.

RECEIVER PIPE. In Mallet Compound locomotives, a pipe conveying exhaust steam from the high-pressure cylinders to the low-pressure cylinders and connected to the two cylinder saddles by ball and slip joints which allow considerable flexibility when the locomotive passes through curves and over rough track.

REVERSE LEVER. A lever pivoted to the frame or the foot plate and connected by means of the reach rod and reverse arm to the link of the valve gear. It moves the link, reversing the motion of the engine or causing the valves to cut off steam at any desired point.

RIGID WHEELBASE. The horizontal distance between the centers of the first and last axles of a locomotive which are held rigidly in alignment with respect to each other. The truck wheelbase of a tender is its rigid wheelbase.

SAFETY VALVE. A valve connected to the steam space of a boiler, which opens at a predetermined pressure for which it is adjusted.

SANDING OUT. See *Real Estate.*

SANTA FE TYPE. A 2-10-2 type locomotive used in heavy freight service.

SEATBOX. A box-like seat used on steam locomotives equipped with a padded seat which forms a hinged cover for the box. The backrest was usually fastened to the rear of the cab.

SHAY GEARED LOCOMOTIVE. A steam locomotive usually equipped with three cylinders, having wheels powered by means of a gear train extending along the right side of the engine. This type of locomotive was usually employed in logging or industrial railroad service where speed was not a critical factor.

SHOE-FLY. A detour track built around a wreck, slide or other obstruction so that traffic may be resumed.

SIDE RODS. A rolled, hammered or cast steel rod connecting the crank pins of any two adjoining driving wheels on the same side of an engine to distribute power transmitted through the main rod to the other driving wheels.

SIDING. A track auxiliary to the main track, used for meeting or passing trains. Also known as a passing track or meeting track.

SIMPLE STEAM ENGINE. A locomotive that uses live steam in all cylinders.

SKIN TIGHT (SLANG). When a steam boiler contains maximum pressure.

SKUNK (SLANG). A diesel or gasoline propelled railroad locomotive or car.

SMOKER CAR. A railroad passenger car reserved for smokers only.

SMOKEBOX. The forward portion of a boiler through which the products of combustion pass from the tubes and flues before being discharged through the stack.

SOFT PLUG. See *Fusible Plug*. Also known as drop plug.

STARTING VALVE. In compound locomotives, a valve operated from the cab to admit live steam direct from the boiler to the steam passages of the low-pressure cylinder in order to obtain maximum tractive effort in starting a train.

STAYBOLT. A bolt with both ends threaded, used for staying the inner and outer plates of a firebox. The staybolt is screwed through both plates and its projecting ends are hammered and riveted over the plates. Hollow staybolts are used for admitting oxygen above the fire and also for detecting broken bolts by allowing steam to escape from their ends.

STEAM. The vapor of water formed by its ebullition when heat is imparted to it. The temperature of ebullition, or at which water boils, depends upon the pressure to which it is subjected. At sea level water boils at 212 degrees Farenheit. At 100 pounds per square inch it requires 338 degrees to boil water and at 200 pounds, it requires 388 degrees.

STEAM (SLANG). Water gone crazy with the heat.

STEAM PORT. An opening in a valve seat or valve chamber at the mouth of a cored passage leading to either end of a cylinder through which live steam enters.

STREETCAR (SLANG). A term applied to diesel locomotives and gasoline propelled railroad equipment.

STROKE. A linear distance traversed by a piston from one end of a cylinder to the other.

SUPERHEATER. An arrangement of tubes through which steam passes and is "superheated" before being used to produce power. These tubes or pipes usually pass through the flues where additional heat is transferred to the steam from the hot gasses moving toward the smokebox.

SUPERHEATER HEADER. A metal manifold with partitions which separate the saturated and superheated steam and to which the superheater units are attached. The saturated passages connect to the dry pipe and the superheated steam passages connect to the steam pipes for delivery to the cylinders or a front end throttle.

TALLERPOT. A locomotive fireman. Also known as *Bakehead* or *Fireboy*.

TRAIN INDICATOR. An illuminated metal frame attached to the front of Southern Pacific locomotives, sectioned to receive cut-out metal numbers, the silhouette providing positive identification of a train by day or night.

THROTTLE. The whole arrangement of valve, operating lever, reach rod, etc., by which the engineman controls the amount of steam admitted to the cylinders.

THROTTLE VALVE. An arrangement or device for admitting steam from the boiler to the dry pipe and then to the cylinders, by which the engine can be started and stopped.

TRACTIVE FORCE. The effort exerted by a locomotive in turning its wheels by the action of steam against the pistons. This energy that is transmitted through the crosshead, rods, etc., causes the drivers to revolve and the locomotive to move along the rails.

TRIPLEX MALLET. A rare class of Mallet Compound steam locomotive used on the Erie and Virginia Railways. They were equipped with three separate engines, one of which was located under the tender. Virginian 700, a 2-8-8-8-4, weighed 844,000 pounds on her drivers, qualifying her as the heaviest non-conventional locomotive built.

TURNOUT. A switch on the rails and fixtures where an auxiliary track leaves the mainline track, usually found at both ends of siding tracks or at crossover tracks.

UNION PACIFIC CLASS. A class of 4-12-2 steam locomotives of the three-cylinder design and used only on the Union Pacific Railroad.

VANDERBILT TENDER. A cylindrical tank mounted on a tender instead of the more common rectangular or "U" shaped or water bottom tank.

VALVE CUT-OFF. The closing of communication between either end of a cylinder and the steam chest. This is accomplished by the valve being positioned so that it closes one of the steam ports. Proper cut-off allows for economical and efficient operation of a steam locomotive.

VALVE EVENTS. The events occasioned by the movement of the piston valves. These include: pre-admission, admission, expansion, release, exhaust, etc.

VARNISH CARS. Passenger cars or passenger train.

VESTIBULED CAB. A locomotive cab whose rear is closed and access to the tender is usually gained by the use of a small door. While the design varies, most cabs of this type also have side doors for entrance instead of the conventional gangway.

WATER GLASS, WATER GAGE. A device to enable the engineman or fireman to observe the height of water in a locomotive boiler. The water level showing in the water glass is exactly the same as that inside the boiler.

WATER-TUBE FIREBOX. An arrangement of tubes in a vertical position with the lower ends of the tubes welded into a hollow firebox ring. The upper ends are welded into water reservoirs forming the walls of the firebox. This design boasts a greatly increased heating surface and allows the use of much higher boiler steam pressure.

WHYTES CLASSIFICATION. A system of classifying locomotives suggested by F. M. Whyte and based upon the wheel arrangements, grouping each set of truck and coupled driving wheels by a number, from the pilot or head end of engine to rear.

Whistle screaming, exhaust flying, silver-faced 4-10-2 departs Los Angeles, California with train No. 831 on November 3, 1951. Steam seen exhausting from bottom of Worthington feedwater heater pump, and from fuel oil superheater barrel just below firebox, indicates that the engine is being worked to capacity.

Gerald M. Best photograph.

Steam
Locomotive
Formulas

Factors of Steam Production

Steam required to produce one horsepower for one hour in modern firebox practice: Saturated locomotive = 27 pounds.
Superheated = 20.8 pounds.

Example: How much steam is required per hour for a superheated locomotive rated at 2000 cylinder horsepower?

Solution: Each horsepower per hour requires 20.8 pounds of steam hence

2000 x 20.8 = 41,600 pounds of steam.

Steam Boiler Horsepower
Formula

$$BHP = \frac{E}{S}$$

BHP=Boiler horsepower.
E=Total evaporation of boiler.
S=Pounds of steam required per horsepower hour (see factors of steam production).

Example: The total steam evaporated by a superheated steam locomotive is 39,600 pounds per hour. Find boiler horsepower.

Solution: $\dfrac{39,600}{20.8} = 1,904$ BHP

Energy Release — Boiler Explosion

The force of a boiler explosion is dependent upon the size of the rupture, boiler pressure at the time of the explosion, and the amount of water in the boiler. As an example: an average boiler having 500 cubic feet area below the crown sheet and steam space of 150 cubic feet, with a pressure of 200 pounds per square inch. At the instant of explosion there would be an energy release of approximately 700,000 horsepower. A boiler the size of those built into the SOUTHERN PACIFIC CLASS and OVERLAND CLASS locomotives would release close to 1,000,000 horsepower at the instant of explosion.

Tractive Force
Two-Cylinder Simple Steam Locomotive
Formula

To calculate the tractive force of a two-cylinder simple steam locomotive, multiply the square of the cylinder diameter in inches by the average maximum pressure in the cylinder expressed in pounds per square inch. Multiply this figure by the stroke of the piston in inches and then divide this result by the diameter of the drivers.

T=Tractive force.
d=Diameter of cylinder in inches.
P=Average maximum pressure in cylinder in pounds per square inch.
   Usually taken at 85 per cent of maximum boiler pressure.
S=Stroke of piston in inches.
D=Diameter of drivers in inches.

Formula: $\quad T = \dfrac{d^2PS}{D}$

Example: Find tractive force of locomotive having following dimensions etc. Cyl. 24" diameter, 32" stroke, 63" diameter drivers, B.P. 200 P.S.I.

Solution: $\dfrac{(24\text{x}24) \text{ x } 200 \text{ x } .85) \text{ x } 32}{63} = 49,737$ lbs. T.F.

110

Cylinder Horsepower
(Cole)
Superheated Three-Cylinder Steam Locomotive Formula

To calculate the cylinder horsepower of a three-cylinder simple steam locomotive, multiply the cross-sectional area of one cylinder in square inches. Add this result to one-half the cross-sectional area of the middle cylinder in square inches. Multiply this result by the boiler pressure (maximum) and then by constant .0229.

C=cylinder horsepower.
c=cross-sectional area of one outside cylinder in square inches.
ci=cross-sectional area of inside cylinder in square inches.
P=Boiler pressure (maximum).
X=Constant (.0229).

Formula: $C = c + \frac{1}{2}ci \times P \times .0229$.

Example — Find cylinder horsepower of a superheated three-cylinder locomotive with 25" cylinders, 225 pound boiler pressure maximum.

Solution — Cross-sectional area of outside cylinder=25" x 25" x .7854=491 square inches.

$\frac{1}{2}$ cross sectional area of inside cylinder $= \dfrac{25" \times 25" \times .7854}{2} = 245.5$ square inches.

C=736.5 x 225 x .0229

Answer. 3,795 cylinder horsepower.

Factor of Adhesion — Locomotive Formula

Factor of adhesion is the ratio between the maximum tractive effort of the locomotive and weight of locomotive on drivers.

A=Adhesion.
W=Weight on drivers.
F=Tractive effort in pounds.

$A = \dfrac{W}{F}$

Cylinder Horsepower
(Cole)
Saturated and Superheated Steam Locomotives Formula

To calculate the cylinder horsepower of a saturated steam locomotive, multiply the cross-sectional area of one cylinder in square inches by the boiler pressure and then by constant .0212. For a superheated steam locomotive substitute constant .0229.

C=Cylinder horsepower.
c=Cross-sectional area of one cylinder in square inches.
P=Boiler pressure (maximum).
X=Constant (.0212 or .0229).

Formula: C=cPX

Example — Find cylinder horsepower of a saturated steam locomotive with 28" diameter cylinders, 180 pound boiler pressure maximum.

Solution — Cross-sectional area of cylinder=28" x 28" x .7854=615.8 sq. in.

C=615.8 x 180 x .0212

Answer. 2,350 cylinder horsepower (saturated two-cylinder locomotive).
Answer. 2,542 cylinder horsepower (superheated two-cylinder locomotive).

Example — Find the factor of adhesion of a locomotive with 271,500 pounds weight on the drivers; exerting 67,700 pounds tractive force.

Solution — $A = \dfrac{271,500}{67,700} = 4.01$

This solution indicates that a pound of tractive effort is produced for each four pounds of weight on the drivers or can be expressed that F=25 per cent of the weight on the drivers.

Other Three Cylinder Locomotives Built in the United States

NON-GEARED

Railroad	No.	Type	Builder	Date	Drivers	Cylinders (ins.)	Total Wt. (lbs.)	Tractive Force (lbs.)	Cylinder H.P.	Boiler Press. (p.s.i.)
Lehigh Valley	5000-5005	4-8-2	American	1923-24	69"	(3) 25x28	369,000	64,700	3,378	200
Chicago Rock Island & Pacific	999	4-6-2	American	1924	74"	(3) 22½x28	301,000	46,450	2,596	190
Louisville & Nashville	1999	2-8-2	American	1924	63"	(3) 23x28	334,000	65,700	2,756	200
Belt Ry. of Chicago	150	0-8-0	Baldwin	1925	57"	(3) 23x28	258,150	66,300	2,856	200
Delaware Lackawana & Western	1450-1454	4-8-2	American	1925	73"	(3) 25x28	382,000	61,100	3,378	200
Louisville & Nashville	295	4-6-2	American	1925	73"	(3) 22½x28	295,000	47,000	2,596	190
Missouri Pacific	6000	4-6-2	American	1925	73"	(3) 22½x28	311,000	47,000	2,596	190
Missouri Pacific	1699	2-8-2	American	1925	63"	(2) 23x32 (1) 23x28	340,000	65,700	2,856	200
Wabash	2604	2-8-2	American	1925	63"	(2) 23x32 (1) 23x28	342,000	64,600	2,856	200
Delaware Lackawana & Western	2201-2225	4-8-2	American	1926	63"	(3) 25x28	397,500	77,600	3,548	210
Denver & Rio Grande Western	1600-1609	4-8-2	Baldwin	1926	67"	(3) 25x30	429,310	75,000	3,448	210
New York New Haven & Hartford	3550-3552	4-8-2	American	1926	69"	(2) 27x32 (1) 27x31	379,000	71,500	3,460	265
New York New Haven & Hartford	3600-3615	0-8-0	American	1926-27	57"	(3) 22x28	245,000	60,600	2,613	200
Union Pacific	9000-9014	4-12-2	American	1926	67"	(2) 27x32 (1) 27x31	495,000	96,650	4,329	220
Delaware Lackawana & Western	2226-2235	4-8-2	American	1927	63"	(2) 25x32 (1) 25x28	397,500	77,600	3,378	200
Indiana Harbor Belt	100-102	0-8-0	American	1927	57"	(2) 23½x32 (1) 23½x28	294,000	75,700 + Tend. 13,800	2,985	200
New York New Haven & Hartford	3553-3562	4-8-2	American	1927	69"	(3) 22x30	379,000	71,500	3,460	265
Union Pacific	9015-9037	4-12-2	American	1928	67"	(2) 27x32 (1) 27x31	495,000	96,650	4,329	220
Union Pacific	9038-9062	4-12-2	American	1929	67"	(2) 27x32 (1) 27x31	495,000	96,650	4,329	220
Union Pacific	9063-9087	4-12-2	American	1930	67"	(2) 27x32 (1) 27x31	495,000	96,650	4,329	220
Alton & Southern	12	0-8-0	American		57"	(3) 22x28	242,500	60,600	2,613	200

Head end view of three-cylinder engine shows the arrangement of the special ALCO designed valve gear ahead of the cylinders. This photograph taken about 1935 depicts the massive bulk of the boiler and cylinders with which this type locomotive was equipped. Notice in this picture that the three valve chambers shared the same axis and then compare with the piston valve placement on the Baldwin experimental 4-10-2.

Richard J. Berry collection.

SOUTHERN PACIFIC RAILROAD
General Specifications
Road Class SP-1

Pacific Lines — 5000 to 5015 inclusive.
4-10-2 type — Named SOUTHERN PACIFIC
    CLASS.
Built by American Locomotive Company.
Schenectady, New York.
1925.
Road class SP-1.
25" x 28" cylinder. (1) inside.
25" x 32" cylinders. (2) outside.
63½" drivers.
225 pounds steam pressure.
Tractive effort, 84,200 pounds.
Tractive effort booster, 12,340 pounds.
Tractive effort, total. 96,540 pounds.

WEIGHTS — LOCOMOTIVE
On drivers, 316,000 pounds.
On engine truck, 65,500 pounds.
On trailer truck, 60,500 pounds.
Total engine, 442,000 pounds.

TENDER SPECIFICATIONS
Water, 12,000 gallons.
Oil (crude) 4000 gallons.
Weight of tender loaded, 291,000 pounds.

FIREBOX
Inside length, 126⅛ inches.
Inside width, 102¼ inches.
Grate area, 89.6 square feet.

HEATING SURFACES
Fire-tubes, 5,286 square feet.
Firebox and combustion chamber, 390 square feet.
Total heating surface, 5,676 square feet.
Superheating surface (type A), 1,500 square feet.
Total evaporative and superheating surface, 7,176
    square feet.

BOILER AND TUBES
261 tubes, 2¼" diameter.
50 flues, 5½" diameter.
Length over tube sheets, 23' 6".
Boiler diameter at first ring, 88 5/16 inches.
Boiler diameter at last ring, 100 inches.

WHEELBASES
Total driving, 22' 10".
Total rigid driving wheelbase, 16' 9". Alco lateral
    driving box applied to No. 1 driving wheels.
Total engine, 45' 3".
Total engine and tender, 88' 4¼".

MISCELLANEOUS
Total engines this class, 16.
Overhead clearance, 195¾ inches.
Feedwater heating system, Worthington type BL.
Throttle, Bradford front end.
Cylinder horsepower (Cole formula), 3,798.
Weight on drivers divided by total weight = 71.3
    per cent.
Weight on drivers divided by tractive effort = 3.80
    per cent.
Total weight of engine divided by combined heating
    surface = 62.
Firebox surface divided by grate area = 4.35 per
    cent.
Firebox surface — per cent of evaporative heating
    surface = 6.87.
Superheating surface — per cent of combined
    heating surface = 20.9.
Factor of adhesion (drivers), 3.8.
Factor of adhesion (trailer), 4.92.

SP-1 (a) indicates that the booster engines were
    removed and the revised weights were as follows:
    Total engine — 433,000 pounds.
    On drivers — 309,000 pounds.
    Revised tractive effort — 84,200 pounds.
    Light weight of locomotives — 392,700 pounds.

SOUTHERN PACIFIC RAILROAD
General Specifications
Road Classes SP-2, SP-3

Pacific Lines — (SP-2) — 5016 to 5038 inclusive.
Pacific Lines — (SP-3) — 5039 to 5048 inclusive.
Built by American Locomotive Company.
Schenectady, New York.
SP-2 built in 1926 — SP-3 built in 1927.
Road classes SP-2 and SP-3.

WEIGHTS — LOCOMOTIVE
On drivers, 317,500 pounds.
On engine truck, 66,500 pounds.
On trailer truck, 61,000 pounds.
Total engine, 445,000 pounds.
Light weight of engine, 395,700 pounds.

MISCELLANEOUS
Total engines SP-2, 23. Total engines SP-3, 10.

SP-2 SP-3 (a) indicates that the booster engines
    were removed and the revised weights were as
    follows:
    Total engine — 436,100 pounds.
    On drivers — 310,000 pounds.
    Revised tractive effort — 84,200 pounds.

All other specifications same as Class SP-1.

Southern Pacific 4-10-2 Roster

Locomotive	Builder	Date	Builder's No.	Road Class		Disposal Data, Place and Date		
5000	American	1925	66107	SP-1 (a)	D	Portland, Oregon	November 24, 1954	OSM
5001	American	1925	66206	SP-1	S	Sacramento, California	March 9, 1953	
5002	American	1925	66207	SP-1	S	Portland, Oregon	June 25, 1954	
5003	American	1925	66208	SP-1	S	Portland, Oregon	July 31, 1953	
5004	American	1925	66209	SP-1	S	Sacramento, California	February 18, 1953	
5005	American	1925	66210	SP-1 (a)	S	Portland, Oregon	December 17, 1954	
5006	American	1925	66211	SP-1	S	Portland, Oregon	October 29, 1953	
5007	American	1925	66212	SP-1	S	Portland, Oregon	March 26, 1954	
5008	American	1925	66213	SP-1 (a)	S	Portland, Oregon	July 16, 1954	
5009	American	1925	66214	SP-1 (a)	S	Oakland, California	June 4, 1953	
5010	American	1925	66215	SP-1	S	Sacramento, California	April 21, 1953	
5011	American	1925	66216	SP-1 (a)	D	Portland, Oregon	February 9, 1955	OSM
5012	American	1925	66217	SP-1 (a)	S	Portland, Oregon	July 28, 1954	
5013	American	1925	66218	SP-1	D	Portland, Oregon	March 2, 1955	DS
5014	American	1925	66219	SP-1 (a)	S	Sacramento, California	July 27, 1953	
5015	American	1925	66220	SP-1 (a)	S	Sacramento, California	June 11, 1953	
5016	American	1926	66788	SP-2 (a)	S	Sacramento, California	May 20, 1954	
5017	American	1926	66789	SP-2	S	Portland, Oregon	May 12, 1953	
5018	American	1926	66790	SP-2 (a)	S	Portland, Oregon	February 26, 1954	
5019	American	1926	66791	SP-2 (a)	S	Sacramento, California	December 2, 1953	
5020	American	1926	66792	SP-2 (a)	S	Los Angeles, California	August 14, 1953	
5021	American	1926	66793	SP-2	Donated to Railway and Locomotive Historical Society March 8, 1956.				
5022	American	1926	66794	SP-2 (a)	S	Sacramento, California	February 24, 1954	
5023	American	1926	66795	SP-2 (a)	S	Sacramento, California	December 28, 1953	
5024	American	1926	66796	SP-2	D	Portland, Oregon	November 15, 1954	OSM
5025	American	1926	66797	SP-2 (a)	D	Portland, Oregon	November 29, 1954	OSM
5026	American	1926	66798	SP-2	S	Sacramento, California	April 29, 1953	
5027	American	1926	66799	SP-2 (a)	D	Portland, Oregon	February 9, 1955	OSM
5028	American	1926	66800	SP-2 (a)	S	El Paso, Texas	August 19, 1953	
5029	American	1926	66801	SP-2	S	El Paso, Texas	March 26, 1953	
5030	American	1926	66802	SP-2 (a)	S	Sacramento, California	May 21, 1953	
5031	American	1926	66803	SP-2	S	Portland, Oregon	September 22, 1954	
5032	American	1926	66804	SP-2	S	Portland, Oregon	May 19, 1953	
5033	American	1926	66805	SP-2 (a)	D	Portland, Oregon	February 28, 1955	DS
5034	American	1926	66806	SP-2	S	Portland, Oregon	May 12, 1954	
5035	American	1926	66807	SP-2 (a)	S	El Paso, Texas	March 10, 1953	
5036	American	1926	66808	SP-2 (a)	D	Portland, Oregon	November 8, 1954	DS
5037	American	1926	66809	SP-2 (a)	S	Portland, Oregon	April 30, 1954	
5038	American	1926	66810	SP-2 (a)	S	Sacramento, California	May 21, 1953	
5039	American	1927	67412	SP-3	S	El Paso, Texas	April 29, 1953	
5040	American	1927	67413	SP-3	S	Sacramento, California	March 19, 1953	
5041	American	1927	67414	SP-3 (a)	S	Sacramento, California	June 11, 1953	
5042	American	1927	67415	SP-3 (a)	S	Sacramento, California	April 29, 1953	
5043	American	1927	67416	SP-3 (a)	S	Sacramento, California	April 20, 1954	
5044	American	1927	67417	SP-3	S	Portland, Oregon	February 9, 1954	
5045	American	1927	67418	SP-3 (a)	S	Sacramento, California	July 14, 1953	
5046	American	1927	67419	SP-3	S	Portland, Oregon	December 10, 1953	
5047	American	1927	67420	SP-3 (a)	D	Portland, Oregon	March 3, 1955	OSM
5048	American	1927	67421	SP-3	S	Sacramento, California	December 2, 1953	

OSM — Oregon Steel Mills.
DS — Dulien Steel Company.
D — Delivered for scrapping.
S — Scrapped.

SOUTHERN PACIFIC 5000 — First three-cylinder locomotive used on the entire Southern Pacific System was beautifully photographed at Los Angeles, California in May 1936. The Pacific Lines operated 49 engines of this type and they were dispatched over all divisions — though designed for use between Sacramento, California and Sparks, Nevada.

Allan Youell photograph. Guy L. Dunscomb collection.

SP Photo Roster

SOUTHERN PACIFIC 5001 — This photograph clearly shows the Bradford front end throttle transfer rod passing through the forward sand dome. The only other such application on Southern Pacific motive power was on the 2-8-4 Berkshire engines purchased second hand from the Boston & Maine Railroad in August 1945. Photo taken in Eugene, Oregon yards on April 23, 1949.

Bert Ward photograph. Guy L. Dunscomb collection.

SOUTHERN PACIFIC 5002 — The fairing located just ahead and above the cab roof drew much of the heat away from the cab and acted as a smoke and gas lifter when the engine was drifting. This was necessary because of the use of superheated steam which was piped to the fountain head (turret) and distributed to most of the auxiliaries. This superheat caused much discomfort, especially when the engines were assigned to the desert districts. Mineral stains on the boiler jacket above the firebox indicate a rare application of the overhead boiler blow-down system.

Gerald M. Best photograph.

SOUTHERN PACIFIC 5003 — Most of the locomotives of this class had their front end throttle connection covered with a dome-like enclosure. This connection, which was just ahead of the stack, is not in place on 5003 and she looks like the original engines in this respect. Flexible staybolts form two vertical rows at front end of firebox. Los Angeles, California, January 9, 1949.

Don Duke photograph.

SOUTHERN PACIFIC 5004 — The big 4-10-2 awaits assignment to drag freight service which will take her across the deserts of California and the great southwest. The original tenders were replaced by larger models with a capacity of 16,000 gallons of water. Photo taken at Los Angeles, California on April 18, 1948.

Don Duke photograph.

SOUTHERN PACIFIC 5005 — This giant SOUTHERN PACIFIC CLASS engine idles away her last days at the huge Southern Pacific facility near Bayshore, California. The amply proportioned Worthington feedwater heater is much in evidence at the center of the big boiler. Solid plate pilot is a later day refinement as are the modified Box Pok driving wheel centers on the main. San Francisco, California, June 1950.

Douglas S. Richter photograph.

SOUTHERN PACIFIC 5006 — Alkali stains on boiler jacket just ahead of the cab are from steam separator portion of blow-off system mounted on top of boiler. Tender carries the old standard lettering of Southern Pacific Lines. Photograph taken at El Paso, Texas in 1943.

Fred A. Stindt photograph. James E. Boynton collection.

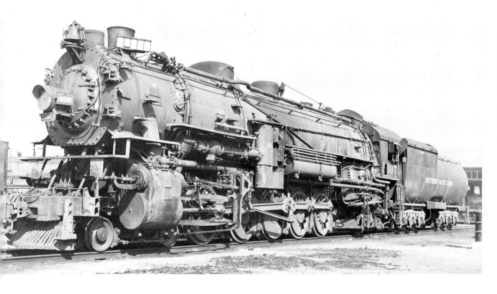

SOUTHERN PACIFIC 5007 — This angled shot shows the details of the front end area of the boiler, especially the old style headlight that was once a Harriman standard. Notice the long pipe that extended from the superheater header (connection just behind train indicator) to the turret valve ahead of the cab. Los Angeles, California, October 25, 1936.

Allan Youell photograph. Guy L. Dunscomb collection.

SOUTHERN PACIFIC 5008 — This locomotive was in the siding at Bosque, Arizona in November 1946, holding a meet with another 4-10-2 coupled with a diesel-electric helper engine ahead. Engine 5037 had just passed Extra 5008 West when her boiler exploded, killing her engine crew and the crew on SP 1333. Picture taken at Los Angeles, California, September 3, 1939.

F. C. Smith photograph.

SOUTHERN PACIFIC 5009 — Hopeful fireboy evidently left Golden State Limited identification on indicator, placing his lowly freight train in a position of great dignity. Tucson, Arizona, January 14, 1946.

Guy L. Dunscomb photograph.

SOUTHERN PACIFIC 5010 — "Brakie" poses on pilot step of this freshly painted engine as she double-heads another of the same class. Engine has a flared stack, which indicates that she is assigned to wide-open-spaces. Most of the class originally sported the clam-shell deflector-type stack, occasioned by their use in tunnel and snowshed territory. Colton, California, October 3, 1948.

Allan Youell photograph. Guy L. Dunscomb collection.

SOUTHERN PACIFIC 5011 — This near perfect locomotive photograph was taken by one of Western America's leading railroad photographers — an authority on Southern Pacific motive power. These engines were originally equipped with one sand dome, but some were later modified and the second dome was added just behind the steam dome.

Guy L. Dunscomb photograph.

119

SOUTHERN PACIFIC 5012 — A freshly painted SOUTHERN PACIFIC CLASS engine was an exception more than the rule. A few desert trips and the glossy enamel was covered with alkali and dust. Photograph taken at Los Angeles, California, July 29, 1938.

Don Duke photograph.

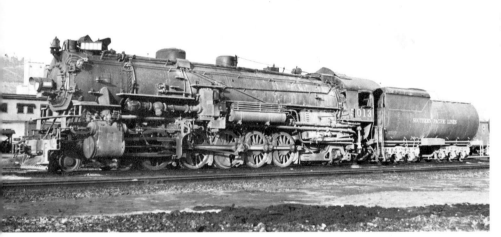

SOUTHERN PACIFIC 5013 — The second sand dome is yet to be applied to this engine and the desert alkali coats the firebox and tender trucks. Pictured at Los Angeles, California, May 1936.

Allan Youell photograph. Guy L. Dunscomb collection

SOUTHERN PACIFIC 5014 — Looking like she just escaped from the paint shop, Engine 5014 exhibits a crease on her cylinder jacket which is visual evidence that she was in a close clearance side accident. Los Angeles, California, August 18, 1946.

Allan Youell photograph. Guy L. Dunscomb collection.

SOUTHERN PACIFIC 5015 — The Dean of western railroad historians recorded this shot of the last SP-1 engine in the series. Los Angeles, California, June 29, 1934.

Gerald M. Best photograph.

SOUTHERN PACIFIC 5016 — Allan Youell could well have been classed with the best of those who captured the 5000's with the "black box." His work was consistently excellent and the quality and sharpness of his photography is evident in most of his pictures. Los Angeles, California, September 4, 1939.

James E. Boynton collection.

SOUTHERN PACIFIC 5017 — The Portland Division used many of the three-cylinder engines in freight and passenger service. Notice the huge crosshead guides on these engines and the lower placement of the bell. Photographed at Portland, Oregon, September 22, 1952.

C. E. Felstead photograph. Allan Youell collection.

SOUTHERN PACIFIC 5018 — Smoke drifts lazily from stack of big 4-10-2 as she enjoys a spot fire on roundhouse lead. Los Angeles, California, June 30, 1933.

Gerald M. Best photograph.

SOUTHERN PACIFIC 5019 — Notice huge open-type Worthington BL feedwater heater and pump with which all SOUTHERN PACIFIC CLASS engines were equipped. This type heater took exhaust steam from the cylinders and sprayed boiler feedwater into a heater chamber filled with this waste steam. The resultant heat exchange offered substantial savings in fuel and water consumption. El Paso, Texas, November 1938.

Fred A. Stindt photograph. Guy L. Dunscomb collection.

SOUTHERN PACIFIC 5020 — Los Angeles, California, March 1938.

Allan Youell photograph. James E. Boynton collection.

122

SOUTHERN PACIFIC 5021 — This locomotive (along with Baldwin experimental 60000) is the only 4-10-2 in existence in America. These two engines differed greatly — Baldwin 60000 was a compound engine with a water-tube firebox. Engine 5021 is begrimed with dirt and mineral, the accumulated precipitate of her many desert wanderings.

Guy L. Dunscomb photograph.

SOUTHERN PACIFIC 5022 — Silver faced SP-2 awaits "highball" on business end of First 934 at San Jose, California in February of 1953.

Robert Hanft photograph. Guy L. Dunscomb collection.

SOUTHERN PACIFIC 5023 — Flared stack changes appearance of the front end of these locomotives. The first engines of this series came equipped with the famous old Sacramento Division exhaust splitter, which was in turn replaced by the more effective "clam shell deflectors." Photo taken at Los Angeles, California, March 3, 1950.

Gerald M. Best photograph.

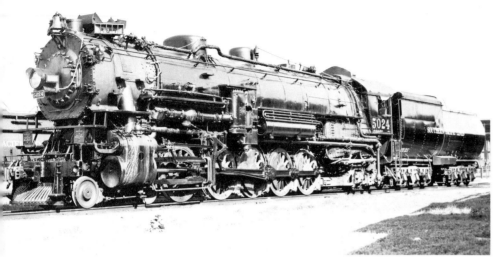

SOUTHERN PACIFIC 5024 — Reflecting the Harriman influence, Engine 5024 is shown resting her three-cylinders at Taylor Roundhouse in Los Angeles, California on November 23, 1934. Stencilling on pilot steps to running boards indicate that the engine valves were set and adjusted in November 1934.

Gerald M. Best photograph.

SOUTHERN PACIFIC 5025 — The original boiler blow-off system exhausted the steam, mud and water underneath the rear of the engines and usually resulted in a whitewashed tender and firebox. Los Angeles, California, November 19, 1933.

Gerald M. Best photograph.

SOUTHERN PACIFIC 5026 — Sand tower in background looks much like the "flack" towers used near Nazi airbases during World War II. Photograph taken at Los Angeles, California, July 23, 1934.

Bill Pennington collection.

SOUTHERN PACIFIC 5027 — Small rectangular housing at base of the sand dome kept water and moisture from getting into sand traps and clogging them. The valve handle extending from the steam dome closed communication between the boiler and the superheater header. El Paso, Texas, May 13, 1951.

Fred A. Stindt photograph. James E. Boynton collection.

SOUTHERN PACIFIC 5028 — Engine is shown standing in front of coal tipple at El Paso, Texas, January 12, 1946. Steam leaks from expansion joint of superheated steam pipe that extends from header to turret valve. Mineral stains sides of the firebox and covers blow-off muffler located just ahead of trailer truck.

Guy L. Dunscomb collection.

SOUTHERN PACIFIC 5029 — Brilliant silver-faced smokebox fronts became standard in later years; this allowing for better visibility and helping motorists separate the locomotive from the scenery. Big "three holer" is coupled to AC Class engine 4293.

Don Duke photograph.

SOUTHERN PACIFIC 5030 — Coupled to a cab-ahead articulated consolidation, the three-cylinder locomotive waits for her crew at Colton, California on January 18, 1953. Many of this class engine were stationed at Colton and were used to boost heavy tonnage trains over Beaumont Summit.

Allan Youell photograph.

SOUTHERN PACIFIC 5031 — In later years the covers that were usually placed over the cylinder heads were removed, exposing the nuts that held the heads in place. Engine also has solid pilot, and notice the rows of flexible staybolts at front of the firebox. Frequent use of the boiler blow-off was necessitated by bad water conditions and usually resulted in whitewashed engine.

Gerald M. Best photograph.

SOUTHERN PACIFIC 5032 — Nicely painted — Engine 5032 is caught with her rods down at Los Angeles, California, March 28, 1941.

Gerald M. Best photograph.

SOUTHERN PACIFIC 5033 — Engine is beautifully photographed in a flood of sunlight that illuminates each detail of her running gear. All engines of this class were equipped with two cross-compound air compressors that were mounted on the right side of the boiler. Photographed at Modesto, California, October 1952.

Guy L. Dunscomb photograph.

SOUTHERN PACIFIC 5034 — Huge printing on tender of this locomotive leaves no doubt as to ownership. Liberal application of oil to throttle compensating level has dripped onto boiler jacket. Photo taken at Los Angeles, California, August 14. 1948.

F. C. Smith photograph. Guy L. Dunscomb collection.

SOUTHERN PACIFIC 5035 — Shown heading First 823 and carrying green signals for a following section, the big SP shows the dirt and grime collected from many hours of hard service. Notice that the bell is mounted lower than usual, and that the asbestos lagging is exposed above the firebox by a missing panel of boiler jacket. Photo taken at Colton, California on January 19, 1947.

Allan Youell photograph.

SOUTHERN PACIFIC 5036 — This huge 4-10-2 was trapped by the flood waters of Tehachapi Creek in September 1932. Her engineer, Alexander Ross, was drowned and Fireman Enos Brown barely escaped with his life. Engine is shown helping another of her class at Colton, California on March 15, 1936.

Allan Youell photograph. James E. Boynton collection.

SOUTHERN PACIFIC 5037 — This locomotive exploded at Bosque, Arizona and is shown after new boiler was applied. American Locomotive Works built the new boiler, and notice that the hinges are fastened to the smokebox door instead of the whole front, as in other engines of the class. Los Angeles, California, May 12, 1951.

Allan Youell photograph. Guy L. Dunscomb collection.

SOUTHERN PACIFIC 5038 — Last engine of the SP-2 class (23) idles at Los Angeles, California, December 13, 1951. Engine is equipped with a Pyle-National headlight.

Gerald M. Best photograph.

SOUTHERN PACIFIC 5039 — Most of the trailer booster engines were removed from these engines because of their never ending maintenance problems. Water marks at base of tender indicate that the fireman has filled tender to overflowing, proving that he has the tank "tamped full of cloud squeezins."

Allan Youell photograph. Guy L. Dunscomb collection.

SOUTHERN PACIFIC 5040 — Engine is pictured on head-end of a 125 car train of sugar beets destined for the refinery at Alvarado, California. A carman's blue metal banner hangs from the pilot beam, indicating that they are working about and under the train. The most restrictive color warns engineer not to move engine or train until it is removed by the person who placed it on engine. Picture taken at Homestead yard, Oakland, California in September 1935.

Guy L. Dunscomb photograph.

SOUTHERN PACIFIC 5041 — Inside main rod on these locomotives was crank connected to the No. 2 drivers. Side rod between the No. 1 and No. 2 drivers was never disconnected on the road. If this was done, the cranked axle of the No. 1 driver would be out of time with the center main rod, destroying the center engine.

Gerald M. Best photograph.

SOUTHERN PACIFIC 5042 — Shown on garden track at Los Angeles, California, August 1, 1946. This was the engine Tom Vernon put into the ditch, nearly killing Engineer Richard Ball and his fireman, Bob Fowler.

Allan Youell photograph. Guy L. Dunscomb collection.

SOUTHERN PACIFIC 5043 — Notice lack of headlight visor. Photograph taken at Los Angeles, California on December 15, 1934.

Gerald M. Best photograph.

SOUTHERN PACIFIC 5044 — Los Angeles, California, August 30, 1936.

Gerald M. Best photograph.

SOUTHERN PACIFIC 5045 — Tucson, Arizona, April 23, 1949.

Carl Rodolf photograph. Guy L. Dunscomb collection.

SOUTHERN PACIFIC 5046 — Here shown double-heading Second 824 with another three-cylinder engine at Los Angeles, California in September 1937.

Allan Youell photograph. Guy L. Dunscomb collection.

SOUTHERN PACIFIC 5047 — Los Angeles, California, March 19, 1950.

Gerald M. Best photograph.

SOUTHERN PACIFIC 5048 — Last built of the herd. Three-cylinder giant has been oiled around by her "hogger" and will soon handle one of her last trains down the steel trail to limbo. Bad steam leak nearly obscures the front end throttle, and the hostler and fireman "tamp" the last drop of water into the 16,000 gallon capacity tender. Los Angeles, California, circa 1938.

James E. Boynton collection.

SOUTHERN PACIFIC RAILROAD
Chronograph of 5000 Series Locomotives

1925 — First of series (5000) erected in April.
1927 — Last locomotive (5048) erected in July.
1953 — First locomotive of series scrapped in February (5004 & 5029).
1953 — A total of 26 SOUTHERN PACIFIC CLASS locomotives scrapped this year.
1954 — A total of 17 SOUTHERN PACIFIC CLASS locomotives scrapped this year.
1955 — A total of 5 SOUTHERN PACIFIC CLASS locomotives scrapped this year.
1955 — Last locomotives of this series (included in 1955 total) scrapped in March (5014 & 5047).
1956 — Last SOUTHERN PACIFIC CLASS locomotive in existence presented to The Railway and Locomotive Historical Society (Southern California Chapter). Locomotive 5021 is preserved for all time.

August 14, 1949, and the 5039 blasts through Milwaukie, Oregon, with the second section of 665.

W. C. Whittaker Photograph

UNION PACIFIC RAILROAD
General Specifications

Road Numbers — Los Angeles & Salt Lake 8800 to 8809 inclusive.
4-10-2 type — Named OVERLAND CLASS.
Built by American Locomotive Company.
Brooks Works.
8000 built April 1925. 8800 to 8808 built May 1926.
Road class FTT.
25" x 28" cylinder. (1) inside.
25" x 30" cylinders. (2) outside.
63" drivers.
210 pounds steam pressure psi.
Tractive effort, 78,000 pounds.
Booster — None.

WEIGHTS — LOCOMOTIVE
On drivers, 288,500 pounds.
On engine truck, 60,000 pounds.
On trailer truck, 56,500 pounds.
Total engine, 405,000 pounds.

TENDER SPECIFICATIONS
Water, 12,000 gallons.
Originally 20 tons semi-bituminous coal.
Weight of tender loaded, 242,500 pounds.

FIREBOX
Inside length, 126 inches.
Inside width, 96 inches.
Grate area, 84 square feet.

HEATING SURFACES
Fire-tubes, 5,132 square feet.
Firebox and combustion chamber, 390 square feet.
Total heating surface, 5,522 square feet.
Superheating surface (type A), 1,505 square feet.
Total evaporative and superheating surface, 7,027 square feet.

BOILER AND TUBES
250 tubes, 2¼" diameter.
50 flues, 5½" diameter.
Length over tube sheets, 23' 6".
Boiler diameter at first ring, 86¼ inches.

WHEELBASES
Total driving, 22' 6".
Total engine, 44' 1".
Total engine and tender, 82' 5"

MISCELLANEOUS
Total engines this class, 10.

Feedwater heating system, Worthington BL. 8809 (Coffin system).
Throttle, dome type.
Cylinder horsepower (Cole formula), 3,448.
Weight on drivers divided by total weight = 71.2 per cent.
Weight on drivers divided by tractive effort = 3.70 per cent.
Total weight of engine divided by combined heating surface = 57.7.
Firebox surface divided by grate area = 4.65 per cent.
Firebox surface — per cent of evaporative heating surface = 7.06.
Superheating surface — per cent of combined heating surface = 21.4.

UNION PACIFIC RAILROAD
OVERLAND CLASS
Historical Facts

8800 — Rebuilt to two-cylinder engine and renumbered 5091 in 1942.
8801 — Rebuilt to two-cylinder engine and renumbered 5092 in 1942.
8802 — Rebuilt to two-cylinder engine and renumbered 5093 in 1942.
8803 — Rebuilt to two cylinder engine and renumbered 5094 in 1942.
8804 — Rebuilt to two-cylinder engine and renumbered 5095 in 1942.
8805 — Rebuilt to two-cylinder engine and renumbered 5096 in 1942.
8806 — Rebuilt to two-cylinder engine and renumbered 5097 in 1942.
8807 — Rebuilt to two-cylinder engine and renumbered 5098 in 1942.
8808 — Rebuilt to two-cylinder engine and renumbered 5099 in 1942.
8809 — Rebuilt to two-cylinder engine and renumbered 5090 in 1942. This locomotive was originally numbered 8000 and carried this number for approximately four years. When Union Pacific took delivery of the other locomotives (9) of this class 8000 was renumbered 8809. All locomotives of this series were eventually assigned to the Los Angeles and Salt Lake portion of the railroad. Rebuilding took place at Los Angeles, California.

MECHANICAL SPECIFICATION AFTER REBUILDING
(5090 to 5099)
Drivers, 63".
Cylinders, 27" x 32". (2).
Total weight engine, 360,100 pounds.
Weight on drivers, 306,900 pounds.
Tractive effort, 72,400 pounds.

UNION PACIFIC RAILROAD
OVERLAND CLASS

Locomotive	Builder	Date	Builder's Number
8800	American	May 1926	66726
8801	American	May 1926	66727
8802	American	May 1926	66728
8803	American	May 1926	66729
8804	American	May 1926	66730
8805	American	May 1926	66731
8806	American	May 1926	66732
8807	American	May 1926	66733
8808	American	May 1926	66734
8809	American	April 1925	66169

Disposal Data

5090	S	Denver, Colorado	March 15, 1954
5091	S	Denver, Colorado	March 26, 1954
5092	S	Denver, Colorado	March 15, 1954
5093	S	Denver, Colorado	March 15, 1954
5094	S	Pocatello, Idaho	February 14, 1948
5095	S	Cheyenne, Wyoming	April 17, 1953
5096	S	Pocatello, Idaho	January 17, 1948
5097	S	Denver, Colorado	March 26, 1954
5098	S	Pocatello, Idaho	November 7, 1949
5099	S	Pocatello, Idaho	November 4, 1949

S — Scrapped.

UP Photo Roster

UNION PACIFIC RAILROAD 8800 — Ready to move through the dusty yard at Yermo, California, big 4-10-2's train indicators show that she will soon head up the second section of train No. 259. The OVERLAND CLASS developed 3,448 cylinder horsepower — 350 less than their Southern Pacific counterparts. Main and side rods have been Magna-Flux coated, an industrial process long used to detect flaws in metals subjected to critical stress. Photo taken March 19, 1939.

Allan Youell photograph.

UNION PACIFIC RAILROAD 8801 — Just like their Southern Pacific cousins, the Union Pacific FTT engines were originally equipped with the Worthington feedwater heating system and all pumps including the two cross-compound air compressors are shown clustered on the fireman's side of the locomotive just ahead of the firebox. Engine is shown standing near the Yermo roundhouse on March 25, 1937.

F. C. Smith photograph. James E. Boynton collection.

UNION PACIFIC RAILROAD 8802 — Long muzzled 4-10-2 wears white flags of an extra train and waits for herder to line "bull switch" and turn her out into Los Angeles yard. Boiler blow-off valves are tapped into the firebox throat sheet and unmuffled jet of water and sludge was blown directly from side of engine with an ear splitting roar and spectacular geyser of steam. Photograph taken December 8, 1940.

Gerald M. Best photograph.

UNION PACIFIC RAILROAD 8803 — Rare bird is caught in the trees of Salt Lake City, Utah on June 11, 1926. The three-cylinder beauty sports the factory paint job and is only one month removed from erection floors of Alco's Brooks Works. Spectator is fixed by engineer's attempt to squirt a few drops of "high speed" on the center engine. Notice brightly polished cylinder and valve covers and the seldom used brass band joining the first course boiler jacket to the smokebox connection seam. An electric passenger car once used to haul passengers to Saltair on the great lake can be seen in background behind 8803's headlight.

Richard H. Kindig collection.

UNION PACIFIC RAILROAD 8804 — All OVERLAND
CLASS locomotives carried Los Angeles and Salt
Lake City initials at one time. These were usually
painted on the cab sides and at the rear of their
tenders. The bells were never moved from their
original location just behind the stack. Photographed
at Yermo, California on March 17, 1940.

Walter H. Thrall photograph. Richard J. Berry collection.

UNION PACIFIC RAILROAD 8805 — This brilliantly
lit photograph dramatizes length of huge boiler
and conveys feeling of the hot desert afternoon.
The Union Pacific three-cylinder 4-10-2 engines
used the dome-type throttle valves and were not
equipped with the steam and gas lifters seen ahead
of the cab roof on SOUTHERN PACIFIC CLASS locomotives. Yermo, California, March 25, 1937.

Lewis Harris photograph.

UNION PACIFIC RAILROAD 8806 — Begrimed with
alkali dust stirred up by her desert wanderings, flat-
faced three-cylinder giant waits for call to service.
Force feed mechanical lubricators were mounted
behind outer steam chests. Southern Pacific mounted
theirs on top of the crosshead guide yoke. Yermo,
California, January 22, 1939.

Allan Youell photograph.

137

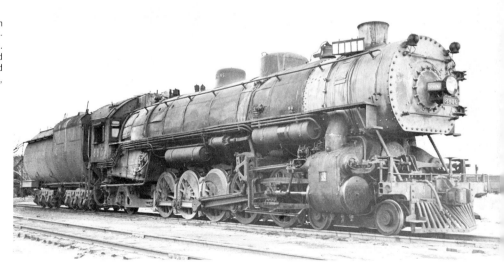

UNION PACIFIC RAILROAD 8807 — This big OVER-
LAND was no doubt suffering from serious symptoms
of metal fatigue as evidenced by the generous application of flaw detecting compound. Southern Pacific-
style train indicators reflect Harriman's former
ownership of both roads. The second sand dome
modification was never made on the Union Pacific
4-10-2's and engines kept the same size tenders
through their long and varied careers.

Guy L. Dunscomb collection.

UNION PACIFIC RAILROAD 8808 — Engine is readied for extra train and last built Union Pacific 4-10-2
has been fueled and watered for her desert run.
Notice placement of classification lights and flag
brackets on smoke box front. Yermo, California,
February 25, 1940.

Allan Youell photograph.

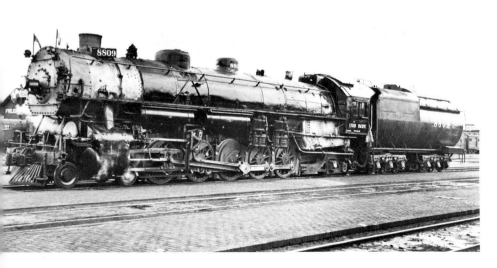

UNION PACIFIC RAILROAD 8809 — Originally built
as a pilot model and numbered 8000, beautifully
painted three-cylinder locomotive waits to head-up
a passenger train at San Bernardino, California on
February 14, 1937. This was only OVERLAND CLASS
engine that went through three numberings and was
finally scrapped after 29 years of service on the big
road. This unusually sharp photograph illustrates
the downward slope of the center cylinder. Engine
8809 was the only FTT equipped with the Coffin
feedwater heating system. The Coffin closed type
heater was flush-built into forward portion of smoke
box just ahead of flared smoke stack.

Allan Youell photograph.

UNION PACIFIC RAILROAD 5090 — Originally numbered 8000, this big nosed 4-10-2 became 8809 when the big transcontinental railroad took delivery of their other nine OVERLAND CLASS engines. The beautifully painted engine had undergone extensive remodeling which included the removal of the third cylinder and related valve gear mechanism. Notice the increased capacity of the single sand dome and the headlight dispersion shield demanded by the contingencies of World War II. The picture was taken at Ontario, California on June 17, 1942 by widely known rail photographer, Walter H. Thrall.

Richard J. Berry collection.

UNION PACIFIC RAILROAD 5091 — Begrimed 4-10-2 idles at Victorville, California awaiting assignment that will take her away from this desert locale and into the cooling influence of the Pacific coastal plain. The OVERLAND CLASS kept the same tenders that were supplied by Alco but the Southern Pacific 4-10-2's later gained tenders of much higher capacity. Small hoses shown protruding from side of tender above the trucks conveyed water to the tender journals when these bearings ran hot. Some railroads equipped engines and cabooses with small portable water tanks used for the same purpose and nicknamed them "Keelies."

Stan Kistler photograph.

UNION PACIFIC RAILROAD 5092 — Shown double-heading with big fast 4-8-4 type passenger engine 822 at San Bernardino, California on September 24, 1947. The huge new two-cylinder castings cover the steam pipes leading from the throttle valve to the steam chests — lending a strange bulky appearance to the front of the locomotive. In later years the engine number was kept permanently on the indicators and extra trains were identified by white flags and classification lights.

Lewis Harris photograph. Allan Youell collection.

139

UNION PACIFIC RAILROAD 5093 — Elimination of the third cylinder allowed room for the application of a rounded smokebox bottom. Structural transformation took place during complete rebuilding at Los Angeles, California in 1942. The main drivers were equipped with Boxpok wheel centers and the overhead boiler blow-down system was employed. Huge ventilator openings on top of cab roof deflected trailing exhaust smoke and gasses and vented heat from back boilerhead. Picture taken at Los Angeles, California, December 9, 1945.

Gerald M. Best photograph.

UNION PACIFIC RAILROAD 5094 — The Worthington feedwater heater has been replaced by an exhaust steam injector which supplied boiler feedwater at a higher temprature. This ideal situation resulted in much less boiler stress and also effected a high saving in fuel consumption because of the heat transfer from waste exhaust steam. Photo taken at San Bernardino, California, November 10, 1945.

Richard J. Berry collection.

UNION PACIFIC RAILROAD 5095 — Alkali staining appears on drivers and firebox side sheets denoting that the huge 4-10-2 has been using water with a heavy concentration of mineral. Constant boiler washing became an all important roundhouse chore in the desert regions. Fireman's blow-off valve is shown unmuffled and blew directly to the side from the mud ring. Engineer's valve was of the overhead type which caused many Union Pacific locomotives to exhibit staining in the vicinity of their cabs. Victorville, California, May 30, 1951.

Stan Kistler photograph. Guy L. Dunscomb collection.

140

UNION PACIFIC RAILROAD 5096 — Notice huge cylinder castings applied to this locomotive after the removal of the third barrel. The diameter of the cylinders and the piston stroke were increased two inches. The engine number plate mounted below the headlight assumes shape of a modified Union shield and the mechanical lubricators have been moved atop the crosshead guide yokes. This OVERLAND CLASS engine gets a cool drink of water from a plug at San Bernardino, California in December 1945.

Stan Kistler photograph. Allan Youell collection.

UNION PACIFIC RAILROAD 5097 — This rebuilt three-cylinder locomotive, as well as others of her class, spent their last days helping trains over Cajon Pass and often found themselves in tandem with Union Pacific's varied collection of experimental "streetcars." Engine is shown at Summit, California and rests her heels after the arduous climb up the heavy grades of the rugged mountains. November 1, 1947.

Richard J. Berry collection.

UNION PACIFIC RAILROAD 5098 — One huge sand dome supplies all the grit necessary to keep remodeled 4-10-2 down on the rail. This engine was originally numbered 8807 as a three-cylinder freight and passenger hauler. Photograph taken at San Bernardino, California, January 19, 1947.

Allan Youell photograph.

UNION PACIFIC RAILROAD 5099 — Last of the two-cylinder conversions, 5099 pauses for a well earned rest at Summit, California between helper assignments. Union Pacific OVERLAND CLASS engines were not equipped with boosters and most auxiliaries were supplied with non-superheated steam. Crossheads were supplied with large guides as were their Southern Pacific prototypes. February 16, 1947.

F. C. Smith photograph.

This new departure from conventional locomotive design was Baldwin's last three-cylinder design. Notice the lack of valve gear ahead of the cylinders and the generous steps and railings leading from pilot platform to the running boards. The cylinder casting differs from the Alco design which were of two piece construction — bolted together to left of center. The Baldwin cylinders were solid cast, and the center valve chamber was set off in a position to receive its motion from the right side of the locomotive. Philadelphia Pennsylvania, 1926.

Herb Broadbelt collection.

Not only the largest steam engines but among the handsomest articulateds were the 4-8-8-4 "Big Boys." Here captured on film extra 4007 west works 79 cars at 20 MPH. Taken east of Lynch, Wyoming, on September 1, 1956.

Tom Lee Photograph

60000

9773-1

BALDWIN LOCOMOTIVE WORKS
Experimental Locomotive
60000
General Specifications

Built by Baldwin Locomotive Works.
Philadelphia, Pennsylvania.
Builder's code — CYZTO.
1926.
27" x 32" cylinder. (1) inside, single expansion.
27" x 32" cylinders. (2) outside, compounded.
63½" drivers.
350 pounds steam pressure.
Tractive effort, 82,500 pounds.

WEIGHTS — LOCOMOTIVE
On drivers, 338,400 pounds.
On engine truck, 57,500 pounds.
On trailer truck, 61,600 pounds.
Total engine, 457,500 pounds.

TENDER SPECIFICATIONS
Water, 12,000 gallons.
Coal (soft) 16 tons.
Weight of tender loaded, 243,400 pounds.

FIREBOX
Water-tube type.
Inside Length, 199½ inches.
Inside width, 96 inches.
Grate area, 82.5 square feet.
Water-tubes (100), 4" diameter.
Length of grate, 138½ inches.
Width of grate, 86 inches.

HEATING SURFACES
Fire-tubes, 4,420 square feet.
Firebox, 745 square feet.
Firebrick tubes, 27 square feet.
Total heating surface, 5,192 square feet.
Superheating surface (type A), 1,357 square feet.

BOILER AND TUBES
206 tubes, 2¼" diameter. 2,775 square feet.
50 flues, 5½" diameter. 1,645 square feet.
Length over tube sheets, 23 feet.
Boiler diameter at first ring, 84 inches.
Boiler diameter at last ring, 94 inches.

WHEELBASES
Total driving 22' 10".
Total rigid driving, 22' 10".
Total engine, 45' 2".
Total engine and tender, 86' 11¼".

MISCELLANEOUS
Total engines this class, one.
Feedwater heating system, Worthington No. 4 BL.
Throttle, front end.
Cylinder horsepower, 4,515. Indicated on Altoona Test Plant (Pennsylvania R.R.).
Combined evaporative and superheating surfaces, 6,549 square feet.
Weight on drivers divided by total weight of engine = 74 per cent.
Weight on drivers divided by tractive effort = 4.10.
Total weight of engine divided by combined heating surface = 69.8.
Firebox surface — per cent of evaporative heating surface = 14.88.
Firebox surface divided by grate area = 4.35 per cent.
Superheating surface — per cent of combined heating surface = 20.9.
Piston valves, 14 inch.
Stoker type, Duplex.
Air compressors (2), Westinghouse cross-compound 8½ inch.
Air reverse gear, Ragonnet type.
Injectors, R. S. Nathan (non lifting) — Special B, 7000 gallon capacity.
Safety valves, 3½ inch Consolidated type (3).

BALDWIN LOCOMOTIVE WORKS
EXPERIMENTAL 60000
Historical Facts

Baldwin Locomotive Work's 60,000th locomotive was used as a demonstrator and totaled about 100,000 miles as such. It was brought to Sacramento, California in 1926, converted to an oil burning engine, equipped with a large Southern Pacific tender and renumbered Southern Pacific Railroad 60000. The big three-cylinder compound engine made several trips over Donner Summit, from Sacramento and Roseville, California to Sparks, Nevada in both passenger and freight service. After a rather disappointing performance on the mountain proving ground, the experimental engine was returned east in 1927. Her last mainline service was performed on the Great Northern Railway at Superior, Wisconsin in 1928 after again being altered to burn coal.

The big 4-10-2 was returned to the Baldwin factory in Philadelphia, Pennsylvania where she was kept in storage until 1932. She was then donated to the Franklin Institute's Transportation Museum in Philadelphia. She was moved through the streets of the city and placed in a hall at Franklin's Museum. The open wall was sealed and the special locomotive resides there to this day as a very special exhibit.

Only one of her type was ever produced for service in the United States. It became evident that the heavy axle loadings on her driver wheels resulted in lack of response by the carriers. Production of the three-cylinder 4-10-2's terminated at Baldwin's plant after the erection of this lone pilot model.

Railroads that operated Baldwin 60000 as a demonstrator: Atchison, Topeka & Santa Fe, Baltimore & Ohio, Chicago, Burlington & Quincy, Great Northern, Pennsylvania, and Southern Pacific.

Locomotive Partially Erected, Showing Completed Boiler

ONE OF A KIND

Baldwin 60000 Test Plant Evaluation

After performing several arduous road tests with her tender tied to tonnage trains, Baldwin Locomotive Works 60,000th locomotive was consigned to Pennsylvania Railroad's locomotive test plant for more scientific evaluation. This famous testing facility, located at Altoona, Pennsylvania, was designed to support test locomotives on huge carrier wheels that revolved in counter rotation to the drive wheels. The energy developed by the revolving locomotive was absorbed and dissipated by tremendous hydraulic friction brakes. This was technical railroading at its best even though it was being done in a barn — the big steamer churning away the miles but not moving an inch. The test plant soothsayer could have accurately predicted the final resting place for the three-cylinder princess by becoming cognizant of her temporary contentment amid the mass of testing devices at Altoona. By virtue of being born a "one-and-only," the security finally afforded the locomotive in subsequent years by Franklin Institute's Transportation Museum building is definitely warranted if not absolutely necessary.

The famous 4-10-2 compound *Prima Donna* made her debut at Altoona chanting a velvety tune of steam and power — her smooth flow of energy negating the addition of the special counter-balancing usually placed on conventional two-cylinder locomotives. This old gal wasn't a "foundation rattler" and her specially designed valve gear and reciprocating parts spun as smoothly as a well-oiled sewing machine. Amid an atmosphere odorous with sulphurous coal smoke and hot pungent valve oil, 60000 sang a song of power that harmonized and blended into a tremendously fluid melody. Temporarily at home, the big experimental revolved merrily for hours under strictly controlled conditions of uniform speed which could be varied at will from 15 to 37.5 M.P.H. as testing required.

Soon the big iron mare roared her defiance at being hobbled by the static testing apparatus and informed the world by tossing huge plumes of black coal smoke out through an iron jack that penetrated the plant's sooty roof. This column climbed high into a gray sky and combined with other clouds formed by Pennsy's famous K-4 engines bent on meeting the challenge of world renown Horseshoe Curve. The blood-shot eye of a reddening sun glowered down on the plant and scattered depressing shards of dim light through the smokey interior occupied by the tethered giant. After the testing began it soon became evident that the plant could not fully hold the potential of the monster engine.

Experimental 60000 immediately showed her prowess by developing 4515 horsepower and would have indicated more muscle if Altoona could have registered it. Under punctilious programming, many important and interesting test data were logged. The tractive effort was charted by a dynamometer, and water-coal rates were measured more accurately than ever possible by road testing. The design and operation of the testing facility eliminated the inaccuracies of road testing which always introduced variations in speed due to grades, track curvature, weather, etc. These variables were eliminated to produce accurate indicator cards showing cylinder power production for given cylinder cutoffs. Combined indicator diagrams for cylinder head ends vividly showed pressure against piston performance throughout the high and low pressure piston strokes at various speeds and cut-offs.

Perhaps the plant officials were not satisfied to force the indignities of hobbling 60000, they proceeded to rub salt into the wounds by trussing the Baldwin beauty in a maze of pipes, test gauges and recording apparatus. Swallowing her pride, the big compound responded by turning with watch-like precision — producing data that soon raised the eyebrows of all involved. She ran a gamut of tests, operating at speeds of 80 to 200 R.P.M. (15 to 37.5 M.P.H.). Cut-offs were tested that ranged from 50 to 90 percent in the center (high pressure) cylinder. The valve gear mechanism correspondingly adjusted the cut-offs in the two outer (low pressure) cylinders from 20 to 70 percent automatically. As an example, the engine was tested at a cut-off of 50 percent in the high pressure cylinder (20 percent low) at 15 M.P.H. using full main throttle. Engine 60000 developed indicated horsepower totaling 1471. The cut-off was then changed to 90/70 and the horsepower shot up to 3034 which was more than twice the value turned up in the first test. This increase could have been anticipated considering that steam followed the high pressure piston under boiler pressure twice the cut-off distance in the later test. During all tests maximum pressures were maintained whenever possible and averaged out to 344 P.S.I.

The indicator card produced when the engine generated a maximum of 4515 horsepower (test 7923) was made at 200 R.P.M. with a cut-off of 80/50 using full throttle. The diagram showed initial high cylinder pressure of 350 P.S.I. following the piston and gradually falling off to approximately 250 pounds at 80 percent piston travel. It was at this point that live steam to the piston was cut-off and the cylinder pressure rapidly fell off to 200 P.S.I. The steam was exhausted into a receiver in the saddle assembly for delivery to the two low pressure cylinders where it was double expanded at 50 percent cut-off. To produce 4515 horsepower, engine 60000 evaporated water at a rate of 83,769 pounds per hour and in the process burned 11,827 pounds of dry coal. The calculated amount of steam necessary to produce one horsepower for an hour at this rate was 14.9 pounds which required the oxidation of 2.6 pounds of coal. During this test the locomotive burned 143 pounds of coal each hour on each square foot of grate area.

During most tests an average temperature of 625 degrees F. was measured in the branch or steam delivery pipe to the high pressure cylinder. The plant personnel became deeply impressed when they found that the boiler and firebox evaporation rates were the greatest seen at Altoona. Carefully charted figures showed that the white heat in the flaming maw generated temperatures ranging from 2400 degrees F. to 2800 at the center of the firebox. While this was a normal figure for most coal burning steam locomotives, an interesting fact came to light. While the big 4-10-2 indicated average firebox temperatures, tests proved that the higher evaporation rates were due to the more efficient heat transfer surfaces. By burning 37½ pounds of coal (Altoona test plant used Keystone Coal & Coke Company's Crows Nest mine run from Hempfield, Pennsylvania) per square foot of grate surface each hour the temperature leveled off at 2400 degrees F. The temperature at the center of the firebox jumped to 2800 degrees when the firing rate was increased to 150 pounds of coal per square foot each hour. The 400 degree increase was out

of proportion to the increased coal rate, but this was borne out by the fact that the efficiency of combustion decreases with an increase in the coal rate. This was the maximum firing rate of the locomotive and it taxed the plant to its limit. At this 150 pounds of coal rate, the firebox and boiler evaporated nearly 70,000 pounds of moist steam which included that saved by the feedwater heater. Temperatures at the back flue sheet varied between a low of about 2000 degrees F. to 2350 degrees. By the time the hot gasses had flowed through the fire-tubes to the smokebox they had cooled to about 600 degrees. Because of her huge size, 60000 had a fully developed appetite for coal and her experimental water-tube firebox required a grate surface area of 82.5 square feet. At the full 150 pound coal firing rate the hungry steamer gulped and then oxidized a little over six tons of "black diamonds" per hour, converting it into heat, gas, steam and rolling box cars.

Five throttling tests were made throughout a series as opposed to measurements taken at full throttle position. These partial throttle tests were made by closing the main throttle just enough to reduce steam pressure (normal 350) to 200-250 P.S.I. at the high pressure steam chest while adjusting the cut-off to produce the same drawbar pull as with a full throttle. Three constants were produced (pressure-drawbar pull-speed) at the expense of one variable (cut-off). These considerations could lead to more definitive tests with more scientific results.

Partial throttling tests proved that closing the throttle to choke off steam chest pressure on 60000 had very little effect on efficiency. This type of throttle manipulation was then indicated to produce minor changes in power production because of little change in economies. Small changes in power production were best made in single expansion locomotives by "hooking them up" (shortening cut-off) than by throttle manipulation. Because the steam was double expanded in the low pressure barrels, it produced additional work and horsepower regardless of throttle position of the Baldwin compound. Machine efficiency varied slightly for throttle reductions and power adjustments supported such operating procedures any time the engine was operating as opposed to the strict throttle regimen dictated for the single expansion engine. It should be explained at this juncture that the big compound three-cylinder engine was also a simple engine when necessary. When the engineer was confronted with huge tonnage trains, he could open a starting valve in the locomotive cab (most compounds had them) thereby admitting steam at full boiler pressure to all cylinders producing maximum tractive effort.

For years the "full throttle whenever possible" theory was expounded by engineers in regard to operating single expansion steam locomotives. Experienced "battle wise" engineers proved that balancing* the main throttle valve on simple superheated locomotives in conjunction with a proper cut-off showed a remarkable increase in engine and machine efficiency. Fuel and water rates lowered appreciably after the throttle balancing ritual was performed. Profound judgment in locomotive management was necessary when running these type engines because steam was expanded once and any error in judgment could not be regained in the act of double expansion. Any steam that flowed under pressure to the stack was wasted potential. Full expansive use of steam was absolutely necessary in the single expansion engine because it was a "one shot deal" and there was not a second chance to wring the power out of the steam. For this reason alone, proper adjustment of the cut-off and throttle was of extreme importance in the efficient operation of this type locomotive.

Some figures from Pennsy's test charts show the following statistics about 60000's boiler performance: At shortest cut-off (50/20) at full throttle, the compound rolled at 80 R.P.M. (15 M.P.H.) on an equivalent run of 33.8 miles. Tender water was delivered to the feedwater heater at 65 degrees F. and was heated to 192 degrees by exhaust steam before delivery to the boiler check — an increase of 127 degrees. Exhaust steam temperature at the feedwater heater was 230 degrees F. and the following temperatures were charted: Branch pipe steam — 568, Exhaust pipe steam — 220, Laboratory temperature 72, Smokebox gas — 519, Firebox — 2415, Combustion chamber — 1980. Comparative figures from a high capacity test are listed in respect to the above low power test. These figures are from a full throttle test using a long cut-off (80/50) at 200 R.P.M. (37.5 M.P.H.) on an equivalent run of one hour or 37.5 miles. Tender water to feedwater heater — 64 degrees (−1),

---

When operating single expansion locomotives under full power requirements, cut-offs were shortened as speed increased using steam expansively. A phenomenon occurred when the throttle was partially closed. Close to mid point, the throttle lever would suddenly become free moving and felt like it was floating. This was the ideal position (balanced), the locomotive speed increased, back pressure decreased and the engine seemed to be in perfect dynamic balance. Naturally this condition greatly enhanced the operating efficiency of the locomotive and in many cases eliminated water stops.

heated to 233 degrees (+41) by exhaust steam temperature of 289 (+59). The re-use of exhaust steam in the feedwater heater system resulted in savings from 7.5 to 10.5% in fuel costs. The following figures are from the high power test: Branch pipe steam 683 (+115), Exhaust steam 313 (+93), Laboratory temperature 65 (−7), Smokebox gas 645 (+126), Firebox 2798 (+393), Combustion chamber 2347 (+367). By reason of higher capacity, higher temperatures could have been expected considering the first test involved the burning of 3,059 pounds of coal each hour and 12,231 in the last.

The evaporation rate of the combined fire-tube boiler and water-tube firebox was also the highest for any locomotive tested at Altoona. While the specially designed firebox evaporated water at a wonderful rate, overall boiler efficiencies were comparable to locomotives equipped with conventional flat surfaced fireboxes. Because she packed 350 pounds boiler pressure, staying of flat firebox sheets in this design was out of the question. The marine or water-tube firebox consisted of mainly cylindrical configurations and this design and planning was backed by the theory that a round sided vessel was capable of containing greater pressures than one with flat surfaces. You might ask yourself — have I ever seen a square oxygen tank?

The Baldwin 4-10-2 was designed primarily to produce high ratios of expansion in the compound cylinders and this was proven by measuring steam pressures at the end of expansion (Two to 19 P.S.I.). This value was lower than for simple expansion engines using lower initial boiler pressure and was the main factor in considering locomotive cylinder efficiency. After all, steam exhausted after being expanded in the cylinder produces no useful work after losing its energy potential in the smokestack.

Power distribution in the cylinders was an interesting test development. At 4500 horsepower — 200 R.P.M. and 80/50 cut-off, the middle cylinder developed 1080 cylinder horsepower. This was 24% of the total and the two low pressure cylinders each contributed an average of 1710 (38% of total each). Amazingly, when the cut-off was changed to 60/30 the total indicated horsepower dropped to 2880 (−1620). The center cylinder only produced 145 horsepower or roughly 5% of the total work by the three cylinders (−19%). The 2880 horsepower test was not truly indicative of actual road practice because the speed and cut-offs were regulated to produce only about one-half the engine's rated power.

Of much interest was data about boiler efficiency charted against the firing rate. This value in percentages dropped as the coal (Analysis of

Crows Nest Mine run: Carbon 74.21%, Hydrogen 5.20%, Nitrogen 1.37%, Oxygen 7.11%, Sulphur 1.73%, Ash 10.38%) burned each hour on each square foot of grate area increased. When burning 10 pounds/hour/square foot, the efficiency of the boiler was at 69%. When the rate was increased to 150 pounds/hour/square foot, boiler efficiency dropped to 52% (−17%). Oddly, this drop as before mentioned was not due to any change in heat absorption which was constant at 82% for all firing rates. The key to the whole subject of lowering boiler efficiency was this — as coal was "piled on," efficient combustion plummeted with a corresponding drop in boiler economy.

The charted water rate curve for 60000 was flatter than for any simple steam locomotive ever tested. The charts showed that it was necessary to supply only 14.2 pounds of steam for each horsepower hour at a speed of 22.5 M.P.H. at 70/40 cut-off. The highest water rate of 16.6 pounds of steam/hour/horsepower was produced at a speed of 15 M.P.H. at 90/70 cut-off and was only 2.4 pounds above the lowest water rate. Compounding the steam demonstrated that the full energy was ex-tracted from the steam (water) at extreme ranges of cut-off and speed.

After full evaluation of all testing at Altoona and on the road it could be concluded that Baldwin 60000 was an amazingly successful locomotive. Why then was the market not flooded with three-cylinder compound locomotives and why didn't America's rail carriers get in line at Baldwin's Eddystone, Pennsylvania plant? When Baldwin built 60000 the design was made with no specific railroad in mind. The actual wheel and axle loadings were too great for the average roadbed and the rigid driver wheelbase caused damaging thrust on tight curves. The location of the third engine between the main frames posed great maintenance problems even though the valve gear actuating the middle engine was incorporated with the Walschaerts on the right side. Experience had proven that the economies effected by compounding of steam were offset by higher maintenance costs and more frequent breakdowns. With this firmly in mind one can readily see why Baldwin's 60000 steam locomotive was *ONE OF A KIND.*

Fig. 3. Boiler

This view shows the openings in the rear firebox wall for the fire-door and stoker, also the relative positions of the upper drums, water tubes and mud-ring. No stay bolts are used in the construction of the firebox.

THREE BARRELS OF STEAM

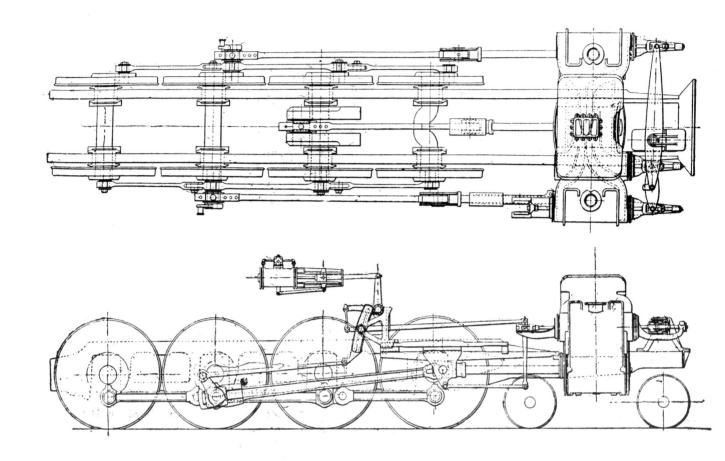

GENERAL ARRANGEMENT OF CYLINDERS
AND RUNNING GEAR
VALVE GEAR, ETC.
THREE-CYLINDER LOCOMOTIVE

General arrangement of cylinders, valve motion and running gear of a three-cylinder locomotive as viewed from
above. Notice the center main rod connection at crank, and
the off-set axle on the number 1 driver which was modified
to clear the rising and falling of the center main rod. Valve
gear is shown in front of cylinders.

Side view of gear and cylinders looking from right side
of locomotive.

American Locomotive Company.

Photograph shows between-the-rail view of crank axle and driving boxes of the number 2 drivers. It was the three-part brass at the rear of the center main rod that turned around the shiny axle bearing surface at bottom of the crank. This bearing was very susceptible to failure, sometimes resulting in destruction of the middle main rod. It is evident that the remote location of this machinery and the almost inaccessible lubrication points was a contributory factor in many engine failures. Even the most dextrous and athletic engineer, armed with the long spouted oiler, considered himself clever if he could squirt a few drops of oil on the focal point of wear. Due to its location, the crank and center main rod brasses were subjected to interminable clouds of abrasive material thrown up from the right-of-way by the action of the locomotive.

Details of the crank axle as applied to the number 2 drivers. The counterweights actually cut down on dynamic augment when the gear was in good repair. The destructive forces pounding the rails were less under those conditions than for the conventionally counterbalanced engines.

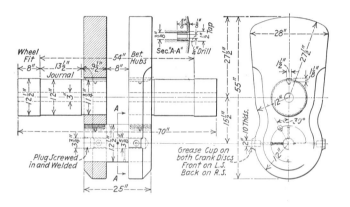

CYLINDER AND CYLINDER SADDLE
ASSEMBLY
Three-cylinder locomotive

A view of the cylinders and cylinder saddle looking from rear of engine toward pilot. Notice the restrictions placed on the design by the center cylinder bore and valve chamber. Most two-piece cylinder castings were bolted together at the center, but this design required this connection be offset to the left of the center barrel. Restrictive clearances at top and bottom of middle cylinder caused its valve chamber to be located to the right, conveniently placing it in line with the center of the two outside valve chambers.

American Locomotive Company

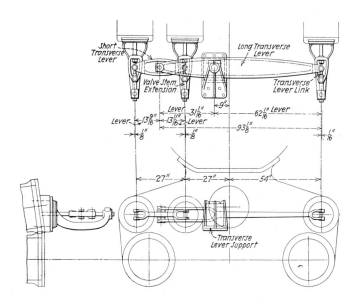

COMPLETE VALVE GEAR. Upper figure shows valve gear as viewed from headlight down toward rail. Left figure indicates side elevation view of valve stem guide as attached to front of piston valve chamber. Last figure shows a cross section, headon view of complete gear as viewed from front of engine toward cab. The transverse lever support was the only part of valve gear not attached to locomotive cylinders.

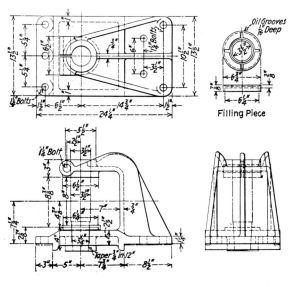

DETAILS OF LINK MOTION
Three-cylinder locomotive

TRANSVERSE LEVER SUPPORT. The support that provided the fulcrum point for the long transverse lever. This was the only part of the special ALCO valve gear that was mounted to the pilot. The lever support had an application of SKF bearings on the main pin.

American Locomotive Company

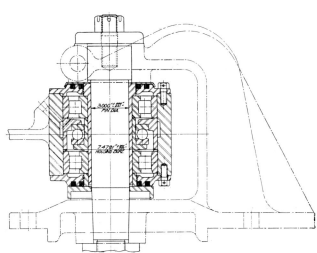

DETAILS OF LINK MOTION
Three-cylinder locomotive

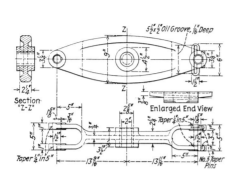

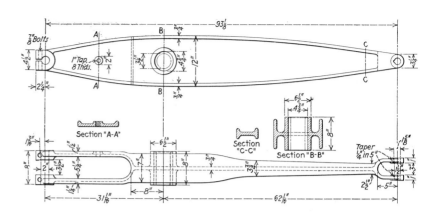

SHORT TRANSVERSE LEVER. This lever connected the right valve stem extension to the middle valve stem extension, and was in turn pinned to the long transverse lever about 1/8 inch off center. It was these close tolerances in the lever arms and fulcrum points that imparted the sophisticated movements required to synchronize the valve events of the center cylinder. With this in mind, it is not difficult to realize the maintenance problems presented to the shopmen who trammed and adjusted the three-cylinder valve motions.

LONG TRANSVERSE LEVER. This lever connected the left valve stem extension to the short transverse lever. This aided the right valve stem in imparting motion to the centrally located piston valve through the short transverse lever.

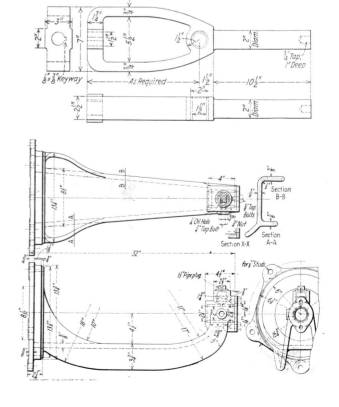

TRANSVERSE LEVER LINK. This link afforded the connection between the valve stem extensions and both transverse levers.

VALVE STEM EXTENSIONS. These extensions were connected to the three valve stems located just ahead of the outside and middle valve chambers. The two outside extensions connected the stems to both transverse levers by means of the transverse lever links. The inside extension was connected to one end of the short transverse lever.

VALVE STEM GUIDE. This portion of the ALCO valve gear was attached to the front of the three piston valve chambers. The valve stem guide supported and guided the valve stem extensions. It is the most readily visible part of the valve motion because of its position in front of the cylinders. This was the prominent clue indicating the engine was of three-cylinder design.

153   American Locomotive Company.

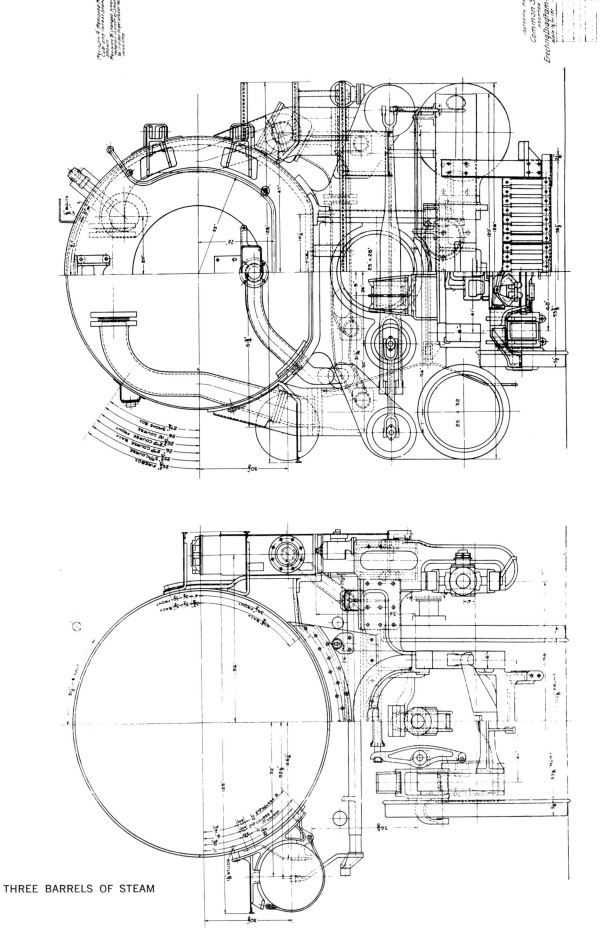

THREE BARRELS OF STEAM

Southern Pacific
Class SP-3

Cross Sections
Scale 3/8" = 1'

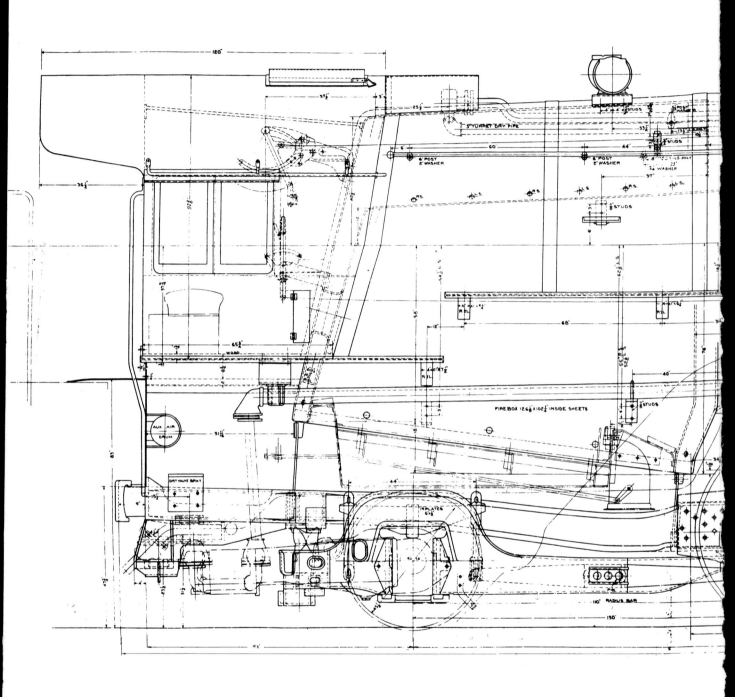

Southern Pacific
Class SP-3

Erection Elevation
Scale ⅜" = 1'

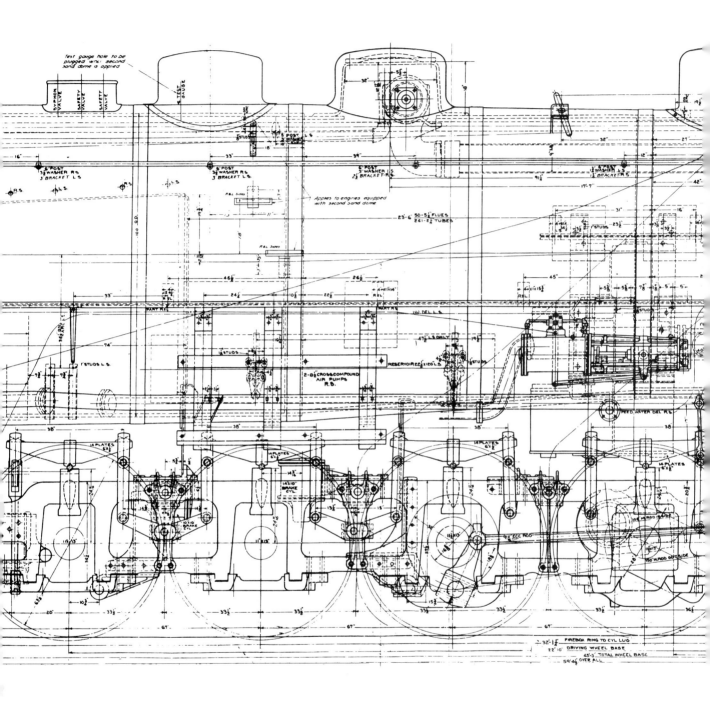

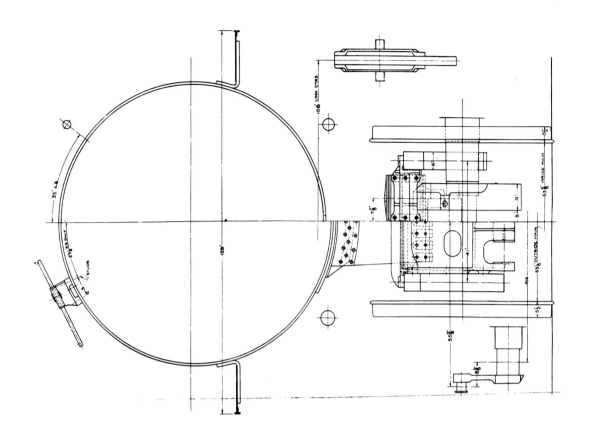

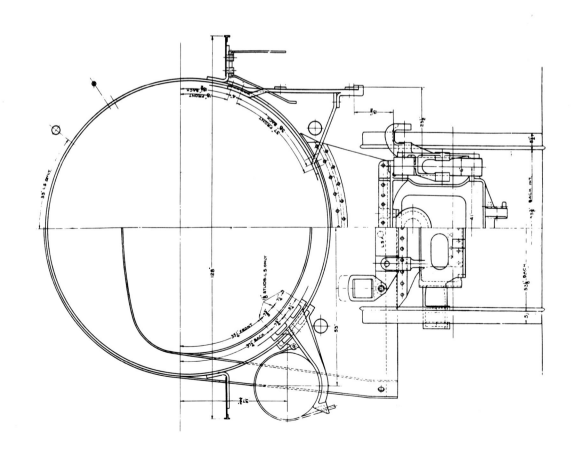

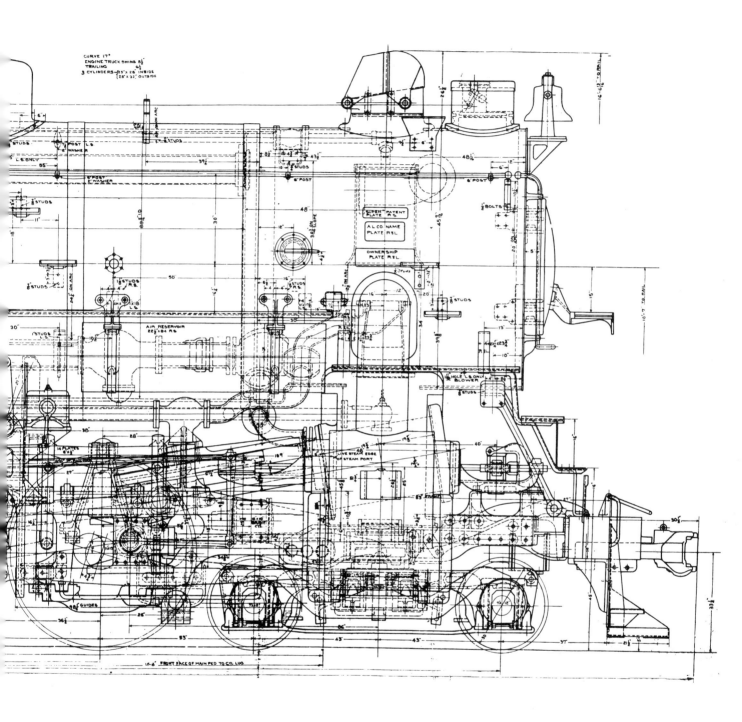

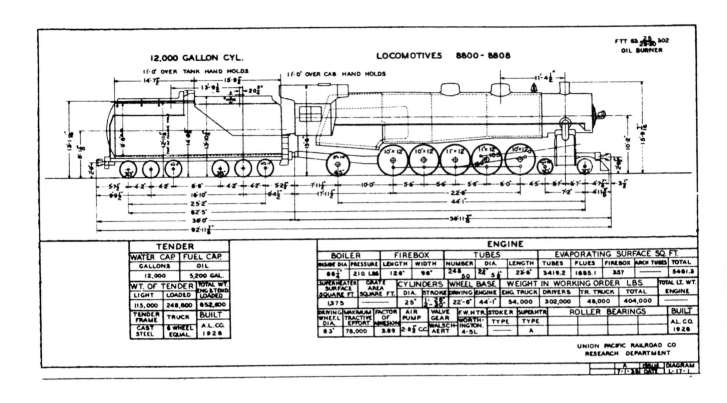

FTT 63 2/6·50 302
OIL BURNER

12,000 GALLON CYL.   LOCOMOTIVES 8800-8808

TENDER

WATER CAP.	FUEL CAP.
GALLONS	OIL
12,000	5,200 GAL.

WT. OF TENDER		TOTAL WT. ENG.&TEND.
LIGHT	LOADED	LOADED
115,000	248,800	652,800

TENDER FRAME	TRUCK	BUILT
CAST STEEL	6 WHEEL EQUAL.	A.L.CO. 1926

ENGINE

BOILER		FIREBOX		TUBES			EVAPORATING SURFACE SQ. FT.				
INSIDE DIA	PRESSURE	LENGTH	WIDTH	NUMBER	DIA.	LENGTH	TUBES	FLUES	FIREBOX	ARCH TUBES	TOTAL
86¼	210 LBS	126"	96"	248 50	2¼ 5¼	23'6"	3419.2	1685.1	357	—	5461.3

SUPERHEATER SURFACE SQUARE FT.	GRATE AREA SQUARE FT.	CYLINDERS		WHEEL BASE		WEIGHT IN WORKING ORDER LBS.					TOTAL LT. WT. ENGINE
		DIA.	STROKE	DRIVING	ENGINE	ENG. TRUCK	DRIVERS	TR. TRUCK	TOTAL		
1375		25"	1-28" 30"	22'-6"	44'-1"	54,000	302,000	48,000	404,000		

DRIVING WHEEL DIA.	MAXIMUM TRACTIVE EFFORT	FACTOR OF ADHESION	AIR PUMP	VALVE GEAR	F.W.HTR.	STOKER TYPE	SUPERHTR TYPE	ROLLER BEARINGS	BUILT
63"	78,000	3.89	2-8½ CC	WALSCH AERT	WORTH-INGTON. 4-5L	—	A		A.L.CO. 1926

UNION PACIFIC RAILROAD CO
RESEARCH DEPARTMENT

A | ISSUE | DIAGRAM
7-1-36 DATE | L-17-1

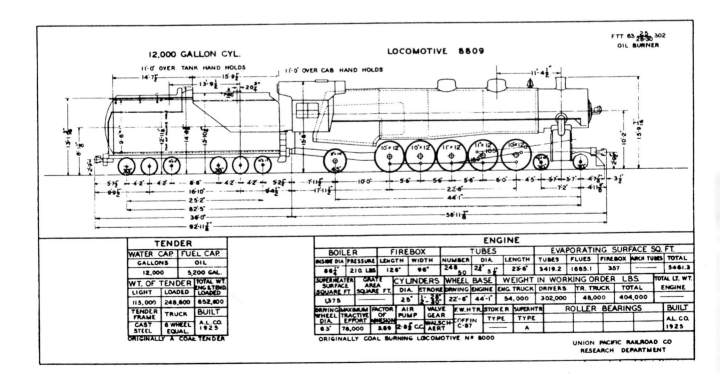

FTT 63 2/6·50 302
OIL BURNER

12,000 GALLON CYL.   LOCOMOTIVE 8809

TENDER

WATER CAP.	FUEL CAP.
GALLONS	OIL
12,000	5,200 GAL.

WT. OF TENDER		TOTAL WT. ENG.&TEND.
LIGHT	LOADED	LOADED
115,000	248,800	652,800

TENDER FRAME	TRUCK	BUILT
CAST STEEL	6 WHEEL EQUAL.	A.L.CO. 1925

ORIGINALLY A COAL TENDER

ENGINE

BOILER		FIREBOX		TUBES			EVAPORATING SURFACE SQ. FT.				
INSIDE DIA	PRESSURE	LENGTH	WIDTH	NUMBER	DIA.	LENGTH	TUBES	FLUES	FIREBOX	ARCH TUBES	TOTAL
86¼	210 LBS	126"	96"	248 50	2¼ 5¼	23'6"	3419.2	1685.1	357	—	5461.3

SUPERHEATER SURFACE SQUARE FT.	GRATE AREA SQUARE FT.	CYLINDERS		WHEEL BASE		WEIGHT IN WORKING ORDER LBS.					TOTAL LT. WT. ENGINE
		DIA.	STROKE	DRIVING	ENGINE	ENG. TRUCK	DRIVERS	TR. TRUCK	TOTAL		
1375		25"	1-28" 30"	22'-6"	44'-1"	54,000	302,000	48,000	404,000		

DRIVING WHEEL DIA.	MAXIMUM TRACTIVE EFFORT	FACTOR OF ADHESION	AIR PUMP	VALVE GEAR	F.W.HTR.	STOKER TYPE	SUPERHTR TYPE	ROLLER BEARINGS	BUILT
63"	78,000	3.89	2-8½ CC	WALSCH AERT	COFFIN C-87	—	A		A.L.CO. 1925

ORIGINALLY COAL BURNING LOCOMOTIVE Nº 8000

UNION PACIFIC RAILROAD CO
RESEARCH DEPARTMENT

Southern Pacific

Detail views of SP 5021 taken at San Bernardino by William McKown are presented here.

Above, a front view of the cylinders from above the pilot deck shows the third cylinder and Gresley valve gear. The large boiler braces show plainly, also the air brake and signal lines on the pilot deck.

Below, left (fireman's) side of the firebox. The booster steam line is the top large pipe. Next lower is water line to feedwater heater, then oil feed line to burner.

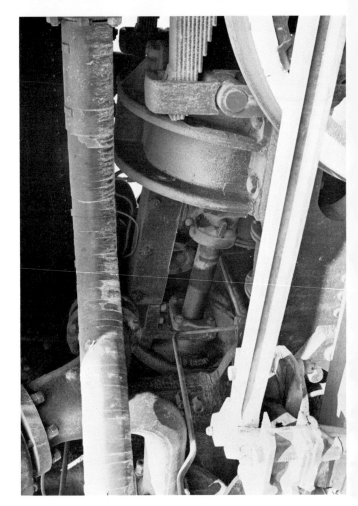

Opposite right are two views of the inside piston rod and back cylinder head. Other views are cylinder and crosshead details, left and right.

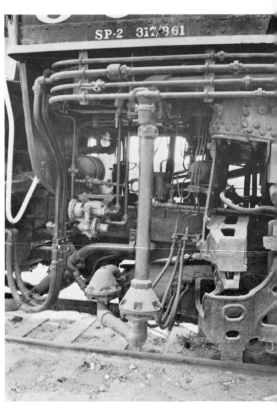

Left, left side front to rear. The Worthington BL feedwater heater shows in middle photo.

Right, under cab detail, left and right.

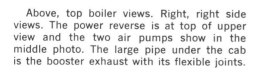
Above, top boiler views. Right, right side views. The power reverse is at top of upper view and the two air pumps show in the middle photo. The large pipe under the cab is the booster exhaust with its flexible joints.

Little-seen detail views of the tender. The four hatches above are for water. Left, steam heat line to left of coupler. Below, air brake and the smaller signal lines to right of coupler.